THE JUDICIAL POWER
OF THE UNITED STATES

THE JUDICIAL POWER
OF THE UNITED STATES

BY ROBERT JENNINGS HARRIS

KENNIKAT PRESS
Port Washington, N. Y./London

THE JUDICIAL POWER OF THE UNITED STATES

Copyright 1940 by Louisiana State University Press
Reissued in 1972 by Kennikat Press by arrangement
Library of Congress Catalog Card No: 75-159071
ISBN 0-8046-1665-5

Manufactured by Taylor Publishing Company   Dallas, Texas

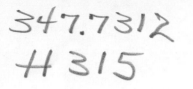
IN MEMORY OF
MY FATHER

PREFACE

ONE of the numerous stories associated with the late Justice Holmes concerns a tiresome lawyer who, after citing an almost infinite number of cases for a proposition, turned to the Court and declared that the Court would either have to decide the case in favor of the plaintiff or reverse the line of decisions he had just cited. This aroused Justice Holmes who, according to the story, pointed his finger at the menacing attorney and said: "Young man, if this court so desires, it will decide neither in favor of the plaintiff nor reverse a long line of decisions, and it will find appropriate language in which to do so." The story is apt in that it describes in a few words one of the major elements of American constitutional law.

Much of our constitutional law consists of a search for appropriate language and of the development of formulae which enable the judges to have their juristic cake and to eat it at the same time. In no class of cases is this more true than in those dealing with judicial construction of judicial power. In those cases dealing with the outer limits of judicial power as marked out by vague glosses on the term "case or controversy," the Supreme Court has developed a ritual and liturgy which it can chant or not as it likes. Through the medium of the injunction it has a device by which it can avoid the difficulties of its own creation in the forms of requirements like adverse parties, sufficient interests, and real issues. Somewhat less monotonous, but equally impressive, is the chant of the Court on

vii

its own independence and the limits on the power to regulate the jurisdiction and powers of the federal courts.

Like most of our constitutional law, that part of it dealing with the courts' construction of their own powers and the extent to which they are subject to other controls presents a mosaic of many patterns and figures; and, yet withal a certain thread of continuity and unity. In choosing and placing the patterns the judge has a great number of choices. By rearranging the figures he is always creating new patterns which blend with the old to form new designs. This mosaic, like the poet's fountain, is "changed every moment, ever the same." The following pages represent an attempt to depict the phantasmagoria produced by the blending of different and, at times, contradictory elements of "the judicial power of the United States."

It is a pleasure to make acknowledgment to Professor Edward S. Corwin of Princeton University for his generous assistance, fruitful suggestions, and friendly encouragement in the preparation of the original manuscript. To my wife, Dashiel Baxter Harris, I am indebted for valuable assistance in the final preparation of the manuscript as I am to my colleague, Dr. Alden L. Powell, to Miss Theda A. Cox, Miss Jane Wilkinson, Miss Loretta Doerflein, and Mr. H. Wesley Ward. I should also like to take this opportunity to express my warm appreciation to the members of the staff of the Louisiana State University Press and especially to Mrs. Bessie Barnett Turpin for their care and cooperation in bringing forth this book.

ROBERT J. HARRIS

Louisiana State University
January 11, 1940

TABLE OF CONTENTS

Chapter I

EXTERNAL LIMITS OF THE JUDICIAL POWER

In a parliamentary government like that of England, where justice nominally flows in a stream from the Crown as the fountain of justice, the constitutional question of the extent and limits of the judicial power and its freedom from legislative control does not arise. Although it is true that English judges have manifested a considerable degree of independence, not to say obstinacy, it is a political fact that in England courts depend entirely upon acts of Parliament for their existence, jurisdiction, and powers. The same is true in France and in most other states possessing a representative form of government where the dogma of the separation of powers must yield to the doctrine of legislative supremacy. Parliamentary sovereignty implies judicial subjection in the sense that it tends to render courts an instrument of the administrative machinery of government without making them politically responsible to the political branches of government.

A different situation obtains in the United States. Under the aegis of a written constitution, which vaguely apportions the powers of government among the three great departments and incorporates by construction the theories of dual federalism and the separation of powers, the courts have achieved a degree of independence from statutory regulation and control that exists in no other country. By judicial decision the term "judicial power" has been gradually converted into a symbol which partakes of mystical and transcendental attributes emanating from the doctrine of the separation of powers and its corollary, the independence of the judiciary. Judicial power, therefore, is difficult of definition. The impossibility of describing precisely the limits of legislative, executive, and judicial power renders any definition somewhat futile. Some acts of government, perhaps, will fall within none of these categories unless one reasons as did the Supreme Court of Errors of Connecticut when it sustained a declaratory judgment statute upon the ground, among others, that the rendition of declaratory judgments was not legislative or executive in nature and was, therefore, judicial.[1]

Judicial power, though difficult of definition, is susceptible to analysis and description. Like due process of law it has been defined by "the gradual process of judicial inclusion and exclusion." [2] The extent and limits of the judicial power are always a question for judicial determination, and they vary according to the time, the peculiar exigencies of the case before the Court, and the attitudes of individual judges.

In his dissent in the *Sinking Fund Cases* [3] Justice Field perceived a clear distinction between judicial and legislative acts. "The one," he stated, "determines what the law is, and what the rights of parties are with reference to transactions already had; the other prescribes what the law shall be in future cases arising under it." [4] Thirty years

[1] Braman v. Babcock (1923), 98 Conn. 549, 555–556.
[2] Davidson v. New Orleans (1877), 96 U.S. 97, 104.
[3] (1878), 99 U.S. 700, 761.   [4] *Ibid.*

later Justice Holmes formulated a clearer and more useful distinction between judicial and legislative acts when he stated that "A judicial inquiry investigates, declares and enforces liabilities as they stand on present or past facts and under laws supposed already to exist." [5]

The Federal Constitution vests "the judicial power of the United States" in one Supreme Court and such inferior courts as Congress may from time to time establish, and it extends this power to nine classes of cases and controversies depending upon the character of the parties and the nature of the subject matter.[6] Whether the judicial power of the United States is limited to these classes of cases and controversies or whether it transcends these limits is a question on which judicial opinion is all but unanimous. In the case of *Kansas v. Colorado* [7] Justice Brewer, in an opinion characterized by extreme verbosity and hyperbolical expression, made sweeping assertions concerning

[5] Prentis v. Atlantic Coast Line R. Co. (1908), 211 U.S. 210, 226. The following quotations are interesting as illustrations of the thaumaturgy of the judges in defining judicial power. "It will not do," remarked Justice Miller in his commentary on the Constitution, "to answer that it is the power exercised by the courts, because one of the very things to be determined is what power they may exercise. It is, indeed, very difficult to find any exact definition made to hand. . . . It is the power of a court to decide and pronounce a judgment and carry it into effect between persons and parties who bring a case before it for decision." *Miller on the Constitution* (New York, 1891), 314. Quoted with approval in Muskrat v. United States (1911), 219 U.S. 346, 356. In Adkins v. Children's Hospital (1923), 261 U.S. 525, 544, Justice Sutherland speaks of judicial power as "that power vested in courts to enable them to administer justice according to law." "Judicial power as contradistinguished from the power of the laws has no existence. Courts are the mere instruments of the law, and can will nothing. . . . Judicial power is never exercised for the purpose of giving effect to the will of the judge; always . . . to the will of the law." Osborn v. Bank of United States (1824), 9 Wh. 738, 866.

[6] Article III, secs. 1, 2, Amendment XI.   [7] (1907), 206 U.S. 46.

the judicial power and declared that the second section
of Article III which extends the judicial power of the
United States to nine classes of cases and controversies
was "not a limitation or an enumeration," but "a definite
declaration, a provision that the judicial power shall extend to—that is, shall include—the several matters particularly mentioned, leaving unrestricted the general
grant of the entire judicial power." [8] "These considera-
tions," ran the opinion, "lead to the propositions that
when a legislative power is claimed for the national government the question is whether that power is one of
those granted by the Constitution . . . whereas in respect to judicial functions the question is whether there
be any limitations expressed in the Constitution on the
general grant of national power." [9]

Such exaggerated assertions of the all-inclusive nature
of the federal judicial power cannot, of course, be maintained. By judicial construction alone the judicial power
of the nation has been limited in at least three ways: first,
by the nature of the federal system; second, by the enumeration of the cases and controversies to which the
judicial power extends; and third, by the principle flow-
ing from the doctrine of the separation of powers that
the courts will perform only judicial functions. Although
the federal government is supreme within the national
sphere, it is a government of limited and delegated powers "and neither the legislative, executive, nor judicial
departments . . . can lawfully exercise any authority
beyond the limits marked out by the Constitution." [10]
The limits of the judicial power of the United States and

[8] *Ibid.*, 82.   [9] *Ibid.*, 83–84.
[10] Taney, Ch.J., in Dred Scott v. Sandford (1857), 19 How. 393, 401.

the scope of the jurisdiction of the federal courts are delineated in Article III; and, accordingly, courts of the United States can take no jurisdiction of a case which does not come within these boundaries of federal power.[11]

The limitations upon the judicial power in the third article also apply to the authority of Congress to confer jurisdiction upon, or vest judicial powers in, the federal courts. Consequently, a statute which purported to expand the judicial power of the United States by vesting the federal courts with jurisdiction in cases not within the enumeration in Article III, section 2, would be void. In 1809 the Supreme Court declared invalid a statutory provision which conferred jurisdiction upon the circuit courts in all cases to which an alien was a party. Chief Justice Marshall disposed of the matter tersely by remarking: "Turn to the article of the Constitution of the United States, for the statute cannot extend the jurisdiction beyond the limits of the Constitution." [12] Before the courts of the United States can take jurisdiction of a case, the Constitution must have endowed them with the capacity to receive it; and, although Congress may fall short of vesting the whole of the judicial power, it can never exceed it.[13] Indeed, the primary function of Ar-

[11] U.S. v. Burlington, etc. Ferry Co. (D.C. Iowa, 1884), 21 Fed. 331, 334; In re Barry (C.C. N.Y., 1844), 42 Fed. 113, 122; 5 How. 103; In re Metzger (D.C. N.Y., 1847), 17 Fed. Case No. 9,511; Dred Scott v. Sandford, *supra.*

[12] Hodgson v. Bowerbank, 5 Cr. 303.

[13] Mayor v. Cooper (1867), 6 Wall. 247, 252. Cf. United States v. Hudson and Goodwin (1812), 7 Cr. 32, 33, to the effect that the courts of the United States can be vested with no jurisdiction but that which the powers ceded to the general government will authorize Congress to confer.

ticle III is to limit the federal judicial power. In *Kline v. Burke Construction Co.*[14] Justice Sutherland emphasized, for the Court, the idea that the effect of Article III "is not to vest jurisdiction in the inferior courts over the designated cases, but to delimit those in respect of which Congress may confer jurisdiction upon such courts as it creates. . . . That body may give, withhold or restrict such jurisdiction at its discretion provided it be not extended beyond the boundaries fixed by the Constitution." [15]

The limitation placed upon the judicial power by court interpretation of the term "cases and controversies" presents a more difficult problem. Whether the strict letter of the Constitution limits the judicial power to a technical definition of cases and controversies is, aside from court decisions, an arguable proposition. It is equally plausible to argue that a proceeding is a case because the judicial power extends to it.[16] Nevertheless, the courts

[14] (1922), 260 U.S. 226.

[15] *Ibid.*, 234. Cf. U.S. v. Burlington, etc. Ferry Co. (D.C. Iowa, 1884), 21 Fed. 331, 334. The metaphor of the Court is interesting. "It is not sufficient that the jurisdiction may be found in the Constitution or the law. The two must cooperate; the Constitution, as the fountain, and the laws of Congress as the streams from which and through which the waters of jurisdiction flow to the court. This results necessarily from the structure of the federal government. It is a government of granted and limited powers. All powers not granted by the Constitution to the federal government nor prohibited to the states are reserved to the states or to the people. The great residuum of legislative, executive, and judicial power remains in the states."

[16] The Constitution simply provides that "The judicial power of the United States shall extend to all cases, in law and equity, arising under this Constitution, the laws of the United States, and treaties made, or which shall be made, under their authority;—to all cases affecting ambassadors, other public ministers, and consuls;—to all cases of admiralty and maritime jurisdiction;—to controversies to which the United States shall be a party;—to controversies between two or more States,—be-

of the United States, from the early days of the republic to the present day, have defined the judicial power in terms of a case or controversy on the assumption that courts can perform only the judicial function of deciding a case or controversy according to an existing body of law. Consequently, any other thing a court does is merely incidental to the decision of the case before it, even to the nullification of an act of Congress or of a state legislature.[17]

What, then, is a "case" or "controversy"? What are its essential elements? When does a proceeding partake of its attributes in such a way as to be susceptible of judicial cognizance? These are questions that have confronted the Supreme Court from the time of *Chisholm v. Georgia* [18] to the present. Their answers have varied from time to time and have afforded vivid examples of judicial equivocation and recondite reasoning.

In *Osborn v. Bank of United States* [19] Chief Justice Marshall, in describing the judicial power, spoke of a

---

tween a State and citizens of another State,—between citizens of different States,—between citizens of the same State claiming lands under grants of different States, and between a State, or the citizens thereof, and foreign States, citizens, or subjects."

[17] Justice Sutherland stated the orthodox view of the power of the courts to declare an act of Congress unconstitutional when, speaking for the Court in Adkins v. Children's Hospital (1923), 261 U.S. 525, 544, he said:

"This is not the exercise of a substantive power to review and nullify acts of Congress, for no such substantive power exists. It is simply a necessary concomitant of the power to hear and dispose of a case or controversy properly before the Court, to the determination of which must be brought the test and measure of the law."

In Robertson v. Baldwin (1897), 165 U.S. 275, 279, the Court stated what it regarded as the better opinion, that judicial power extended "only to the trial and determination of 'cases' in courts of record."

[18] (1793), 2 Dall. 419.   [19] (1824), 9 Wh. 738.

case as arising when a party asserted his rights "in the form prescribed by law." [20] This conception of the term "case" was a broad one and left to Congress a wide discretion in defining it. Since the Chief Justice was attempting, throughout his opinion, to justify the statute permitting the bank to sue in the federal courts, it is a logical inference that he was thinking of statutes when he spoke of a case arising when a party asserted his rights in the forms prescribed by law.

In 1887 Justice Field, while on circuit, attempted to settle once and for all time the meaning of "cases and controversies." Relying upon *Chisholm v. Georgia* [21] and Tucker's edition of Blackstone, he reiterated the idea that if the term "controversies" is distinguishable from "cases," the reason is that it includes only suits of a civil nature. Then he proceeded to elaborate Marshall's description of a case. "By cases and controversies," he said, "are intended the claims of litigants brought before the courts for determination by such regular proceedings as are established by law or custom for the protection or enforcement of rights, or the prevention, redress, or punishment of wrongs. Whenever the claim of a party under the Constitution, laws, or treaties of the United States takes such a form that the judicial power is capable of acting upon it, then it has become a case. The term implies the existence of present or possible adverse parties whose contentions are submitted to the court for adjudication." [22]

---

[20] *Ibid.*, 818–819.   [21] (1793), 2 Dall. 419, 431, 432.
[22] In re Pacific Ry. Commission (C.C., N.D., Cal., 1887), 32 Fed. 241, 255. Field repeated the substance of this definition in Smith v. Adams (1889), 130 U.S. 167, 173–174, citing and quoting Osborn v. Bank of U.S. (1824), 9 Wh. 738, 819, as authority.

Thus far, save for his emphasis upon adverse parties, Justice Field's definition does not differ materially from that of Chief Justice Marshall. Even in that particular it was a contingent, not an absolute adversity, that he emphasized. His conclusion, however, echoed some earlier views of the Court and heralded others that were to follow. "By extending the judicial power to all cases in law and equity," he continued, quoting from Story, "the Constitution has never been understood to confer on that department any political power whatever. To come within this description, a question must assume a legal form for forensic litigation and judicial decision. There must be parties to come into court, who can be reached by its process, and bound by its power, whose rights admit of ultimate decision by a tribunal to which they are bound to submit." [23]

In *Muskrat v. United States* [24] the Court adopted the views of both Marshall and Field and proceeded to rule that the exercise of the judicial power was limited to cases and controversies. Accordingly, an act of Congress authorizing certain Indians to bring suits against the United States to test the validity of the Indian allotment acts was pronounced void because the questions involved were not presented in a case or controversy and because the Supreme Court was held to have no substantive power to declare acts of Congress unconstitutional. By combining the views of Marshall and Field and then enunciating the rule that the judicial power is limited by the term "cases and controversies," the Court was guilty of three contradictions. Although Marshall stated clearly

[23] In re Pacific Ry. Commission, *supra,* 56.
[24] (1911), 219 U.S. 346.

that the judicial power is capable of acting only when a party asserts his rights in the forms prescribed by law, he was merely stating the general principle that courts cannot take the initiative in adjudicating controverted questions but must wait until they are duly presented to the Court for its determination. Assuming, however, that Marshall did intend to limit the judicial power by juridical refinements of the word "cases," that limitation meant but little because of the discretion left in Congress to prescribe the legal forms in which a party could assert his rights.

In Field's opinion we get a different view; but cases are defined in terms of judicial power and not the judicial power in the terms of cases. A proceeding is a case because the judicial power extends to it. The *Muskrat* case reverses this process and defines judicial power in the terms of cases and controversies to which are attached certain esoteric connotations known only to the judicial mind. The total result of such tautologies and subtleties is that whether a proceeding is a case within the meaning of the Constitution is a question for judicial determination and not legislative definition.

The decision in the *Muskrat* case rests on two grounds: first, the nature of the power; and second, the meaning of the word "case." Adopting Justice Miller's definition of the judicial power as that of "a court to decide and pronounce a judgment and carry it into effect between persons and parties who bring a case before it for decision," [25] the Court proceeded to declare that such

[25] *Miller on the Constitution*—quoted, approvingly, at p. 356. The Court elsewhere defined the judicial power of the United States, as the "right to determine actual controversies arising between adverse litigants, duly instituted in courts of proper jurisdiction." P. 361.

power was limited to cases and controversies. Applying the tests prescribed in the opinion of Chief Justice Marshall [26] and Justice Field,[27] the Court found that the proceedings initiated by Muskrat and others were not cases or controversies on the grounds that they were attempts to obtain a judicial declaration of the validity of an act of Congress, that the United States had no interest adverse to the claimants, and that the Court could not render a judgment that would conclude private parties in actual litigation involving the validity of the acts. The language of the opinion is interesting and deserves quotation at length:

> This attempt to obtain a judicial declaration of the validity of the act of Congress is not presented in a "case" or "controversy," to which, under the Constitution of the United States, the judicial power alone extends. It is true the United States is made a defendant to this action, but it has not interest adverse to the claimants. The object is not to assert a property right as against the Government, or to demand compensation for alleged wrongs because of action upon its part. The whole purpose of the law is to determine the constitutional validity of this class of legislation, in a suit not arising between parties concerning a property right necessarily involved in the decision in question, but in a proceeding against the Government in its sovereign capacity, and concerning which the only judgment required is to settle the doubtful character of the legislation in question. . . . If such actions as are here attempted, to determine the validity of legislation, are sustained, the result will be that this Court,

[26] Marbury v. Madison (1803), 1 Cr. 137, where the Chief Justice defined "case" as a suit instituted according to the regular course of judicial procedure; Osborn v. Bank of U.S. (1824), 9 Wh. 738, 819; Cohens v. Virginia (1821), 6 Wh. 264, quoted at pp. 356, 357, 358.

[27] In re Pacific Ry. Commission (1887), 32 Fed. 241, 255, quoted at pp. 356–357.

instead of keeping within the limits of judicial power and deciding cases or controversies arising between opposing parties, as the Constitution intended it should, will be required to give opinions in the nature of advice concerning legislative action, a function never conferred upon it by the Constitution, and against the exercise of which this Court has steadily set its face from the beginning.[28]

Justice Day's definition of judicial power as "the right to determine actual controversies arising between adverse litigants duly instituted in courts of proper jurisdiction" leads to some serious difficulties. Further complications are introduced in the concepts of actual controversies, adverse litigants, and substantial interest. How much adversity must exist before a controversy becomes actual? How substantial must the interests of the parties be? How far may the legislature go in prescribing forms by which suits are brought? These are the questions raised along with the other one—what functions are strictly judicial or, perhaps better, what functions are nonjudicial in their nature?

The concepts "adverse parties," "real interests," and "actual controversies" are often inseparable and will be considered together. They arise for the most part in cases where a determination of a constitutional question is sought, where equity is resorted to for the purpose of securing a declaration of rights, and where political questions and disputes between sovereignties are involved. In all of these classes of cases the courts have developed certain doctrines which tend to limit the judicial power and prevent judicial usurpation. Thus, where the constitutionality of a statute is involved, the Supreme Court

[28] Muskrat v. U.S. (1911), 219 U.S. 346, 361–362.

insists that the issue must be raised in an actual controversy by competent parties who have substantial adverse interests at stake.[29] This is but a corollary of the broader doctrine of the Supreme Court that it has no substantive power to declare legislative enactments void but merely the power to declare the law for particular cases as they arise.[30] Similarly, in suits in equity the courts have laid down the rule that there must be a real controversy in which there is an actual wrong or threat of wrong.[31] Finally, the courts of the United States are not to determine political questions and are, therefore, cautious against taking jurisdiction in disputes between sovereignties over the possession of political power,[32] and disputes between states, or to which a state is a party, concerning nonjusticiable issues.[33]

Greater emphasis seems to be placed on the necessity of adverse parties with substantial interests in proceedings where the validity of the statute or order is questioned than in the other classes. The general rule is well stated in *Chicago and Grand Trunk R. Co. v. Wellman*,[34] which originated in the Michigan courts upon an agreed statement of facts between friendly parties who desired to contest the validity of a statute regulating passenger rates. The Supreme Court of the United States

[29] Chicago and Grand Trunk R. Co. v. Wellman (1892), 143 U.S. 339, 344–345; Muskrat v. U.S. (1911), 219 U.S. 346.

[30] Adkins v. Children's Hospital (1923), 261 U.S. 525; Muskrat v. U.S. (1911), 219 U.S. 346; Marbury v. Madison (1803), 1 Cr. 137.

[31] Willing v. Chicago Auditorium Ass'n (1928), 277 U.S. 274, 288, 289. Cf. Brandeis' dissent in Pennsylvania and Ohio v. West Virginia (1923), 262 U.S. 553, 610–615.

[32] Luther v. Borden (1849), 7 How. 1.

[33] Massachusetts v. Mellon (1923), 262 U.S. 447.

[34] (1892), 143 U.S. 339.

affirmed the holdings of the Michigan courts and, after pointing out that the courts had no "immediate and general supervision of the constitutionality" of legislative acts, said:

Whenever in pursuance of an honest and actual antagonistic assertion of rights by one individual against another, there is presented a question involving the validity of any act of any legislature, State or Federal, and the decision necessarily rests on the competency of the legislature to so enact, the court must, in the exercise of its solemn duties, determine whether the act be constitutional or not; but such an exercise of power is the ultimate and supreme function of courts. It is legitimate only in the last resort, and as a necessity in the determination of real, earnest and vital controversy between individuals. It never was the thought that, by means of a friendly suit, a party beaten in the legislature could transfer to the courts an inquiry as to the constitutionality of the legislative act.[35]

Objection to the validity of a statute, therefore, must be raised by one adversely affected and not by a stranger to its operation.[36] The interest must be of a personal and not of an official nature.[37] Accordingly, a county court cannot contest the validity of a statute merely in the interest of third parties,[38] nor a county auditor contest the validity of a tax exemption statute although he is charged with its enforcement,[39] nor can directors of an irrigation district occupy a position antagonistic to the district.[40]

[35] Ibid., 345.

[36] Lampasas v. Bell (1901), 180 U.S. 276, 284, where it was held in a suit to recover interest on bonds that a municipality had no interest in the validity of an act of incorporation.

[37] Braxton County Court v. State of West Va. (1908), 208 U.S. 192.

[38] Ibid., 198.

[39] Smith v. Indiana ex rel. Lewis (1903), 191 U.S. 138, 149.

[40] Tregea v. Modesto Irrigation District (1896), 164 U.S. 179. See

The interest of a party contesting the validity of a statute must be direct. Thus employers have no interest adversely affected by an alleged denial of equal protection of the laws to employees under a workmen's compensation statute.[41]

The leading case is *Marye v. Parsons*,[42] one of the famous *Virginia Coupon Cases*, where a bill was filed by a citizen of New York against the auditor of Virginia and others to compel specific performance of alleged contracts by accepting overdue bonds held by him as payment for taxes for any taxpayer presenting them. The order was granted; but upon appeal the Supreme Court held that the bill should have been dismissed because of the petitioner's lack of interest in the contract in so far as the petitioner had no taxes to pay, and his interest would cease after such transfer in spite of the fact that the act in question tended to destroy the value of the bonds. Justice Matthews said, speaking for himself and four of his associates:

The bill, as framed, therefore, calls for a declaration of an abstract character, that the contract set out requiring coupons to be received in payment of taxes and debts due to the state is valid; that the statutes of the General Assembly of Virginia impairing its obligations are contrary to the Constitution of the United States, and therefore void; and that it is the legal duty of the collecting officers of the state to receive them when offered in payment of such debts and taxes.

---

also Tyler v. Judges (1900), 179 U.S. 405; Clark v. Kansas City (1900), 176 U.S. 144, 188; Ludeling v. Chaffe (1892), 143 U.S. 301; Giles v. Little (1890), 134 U.S. 645.

[41] Jeffrey Mfg. Co. v. Blagg (1915), 235 U.S. 571; cf. Hendricks v. Maryland (1915), 235 U.S. 611, 621.

[42] (1884), 114 U.S. 325.

But no court sits to determine questions of law *in thesi*. There must be a litigation upon actual transactions between real parties, growing out of a controversy affecting legal or equitable rights as to person or property. All questions of law arising in such cases are judicially determinable. The present is not a case of that description.[43]

In line with this ruling are *Frothingham v. Mellon* [44] and *Williams v. Riley*.[45] In the former case it was held that a taxpayer of the United States could not maintain a suit to enjoin expenditure of public funds because the interest of such a taxpayer in the public money "is shared with millions of others; is comparatively minute and indeterminable; and the effect upon future taxation, of any payment out of the funds, so remote, fluctuating, and uncertain, that no basis is afforded for an appeal to the preventive powers of a court of equity." [46] Moreover, under the separation of powers the judiciary is confined to the duty of interpreting and applying the laws in cases properly brought before the courts and has no power per se to review statutes on the ground of unconstitutionality. Accordingly, to prevent the executive department from enforcing an act of Congress asserted to be unconstitutional "would be not to decide a judicial controversy, but to assume a position of authority over the governmental acts of another and co-equal department, an authority which plainly we do not possess." [47]

[43] *Ibid.*, 329–330. Waite, Ch.J., and Miller, Bradley, and Gray, J.J. dissenting, but with no reference to adversity of interests and competency of the parties.

[44] (1923), 262 U.S. 447.   [45] (1929), 280 U.S. 78.

[46] (1923), 262 U.S. 447, 487.

[47] *Ibid.*, 488–489. Courts sometimes advert to their real reasons for a particular decision in their opinions. Perhaps the following was not

In *Williams v. Riley* the interest of the taxpayer was more direct. Here a taxpayer had brought suit to enjoin the collection of a gasoline tax. Relying on the *Frothingham* case, the Court ruled that the operator of motor vehicles could not maintain such a suit because the validity of state legislation could be considered only when "the justification for some direct injury suffered or threatened, presenting a justiciable controversy, is made to rest upon such an act." [48]

A few cases may be noted briefly. In *Stearns v. Wood* [49] a bill was filed by an officer in the Ohio National Guard which alleged that if certain orders of the Secretary of War fixing maximum ranks in the National Guard were executed, he would be deprived of his opportunity of attaining and serving in the higher rank permitted by state law. The bill also sought a construction of certain sections of the Constitution, the powers of the national government over the National Guard, and the authority to use it without the territorial limits of the United States. The language of the Court, speaking through Justice McReynolds, is interesting:

---

the least motive in guiding the Court to its conclusion here: "If one taxpayer may champion and litigate such a cause, then every other taxpayer may do the same, not only in respect of the statute here under review but also in respect of every other appropriation act and statute whose administration requires the outlay of public money, and whose validity may be questioned. The bare suggestion of such a result, with its attendant inconveniences, goes far to sustain the conclusion which we have reached, that a suit of this character cannot be maintained." P. 487.

[48] (1929), 280 U.S. 78, 80. Taft, Ch.J., and Van Devanter and Butler, J.J., were of the opinion that the status of appellants entitled them to maintain the suit but that the decree should have been affirmed.

[49] (1915), 236 U.S. 75.

The general orders referred to in the bill do not directly violate or threaten interference with the personal rights of appellant—a major in the National Guard, whose present rank remains undisturbed. He is not therefore in position to question their validity; and certainly he may not demand that we construe orders, Acts of Congress, and the Constitution, for the information of himself and others, notwithstanding their laudable feeling of deep interest in the subject. The province of courts is to decide real controversies, not to discuss abstract propositions.[50]

Fairchild v. Hughes,[51] like *Stearns v. Wood*, is another manifestation of highly developed litigious instincts. This was a suit to restrain the Secretary of State of the United States from proclaiming the ratification of the Nineteenth Amendment and the Attorney General from enforcing it. The suit, of course, was dismissed because it was not regarded as a case within the meaning of the judicial article. The Court reasoned that the general right of the private citizen to have the government administered according to law and to prevent wasting of public moneys did not entitle him to institute in the federal courts a suit to secure a determination whether a statute if passed or enforced, or a constitutional amendment about to be adopted, would be valid.[52] Likewise in *Ex parte Levitt* [53] the Court denied a motion of an attorney for leave to file a petition for an order requiring Justice Black to show cause why he should be permitted to serve as an associate justice of the Supreme Court. The Court found no showing of immediate danger to Levitt from the appointment and declared that it was

[50] *Ibid.*, 78.   [51] (1922), 258 U.S. 126.
[52] *Ibid.*, 129–130. Cf. Giles v. Harris (1903), 189 U.S. 475; Tyler v. Judges (1900), 179 U.S. 405.
[53] (1937), 302 U.S. 633.

"not sufficient" that he had "merely a general interest common to all members of the public."

In other cases, however, the Court has upheld the jurisdiction of the lower courts in enjoining the enforcement of legislation at the behest of parties who would seem to have had no more direct interests than some of those who were denied relief in the cases dismissed above. In *Pollock v. Farmers' Loan and Trust Co.* [54] the jurisdiction of a federal district court in enjoining the payment of an income tax was sustained in spite of the fact that the suit was brought by a stockholder to restrain a corporation from paying the tax. A similar situation arose twenty years later in the *Brushaber* case,[55] and again the courts took cognizance of the suit as a duly instituted case. To find adversity in such cases requires the imagination to picture tax-loving corporations rushing avidly to pay high corporate taxes to the government against the interests and wishes of its shareholders, but the courts found it and took jurisdiction.

Indeed, injunction suits brought by stockholders against corporations have proved to be a most useful instrument to test the validity of legislation when it is otherwise difficult to present constitutional questions to the Court. Such suits provide the Court with a lever by which it may extricate itself from difficulties of its own creation whenever it desires to pass upon constitutional issues. The utility of such a lever is well illustrated in *Smith v. Kansas City Title Co.*[56] and *Ashwander v. Tennessee Valley Authority.*[57]

[54] (1895), 157 U.S. 429.
[55] Brushaber v. Union Pacific Railroad Co. (1916), 240 U.S. 1.
[56] (1921), 255 U.S. 180.   [57] (1936), 297 U.S. 288.

In the former case the Supreme Court ruled that the constitutional issue of the validity of the amended farm loan act of 1916 was properly presented in a bill brought by a stockholder to restrain the title company from investing its funds in farm loan bonds issued by the federal land banks created by the act. The Court found its escape from the requirement of adverse parties in the prohibition of the company's charter against investing in governmental securities, the issue of which was not authorized by a valid statute.[58]

In the *Ashwander* case the judges appear in all the splendor of a medicine man at a tribal celebration. Here was a case involving not only the huge economic interest of privately owned electric power companies, but also conflicting theories of government and tense emotional clashes. With elaborate ceremony the Court celebrated the ideals of the federal system and limited government and, above all, the ideal of a judicial system that has no substantive power to annul an act of Congress but only the power to declare the law as it exists when a case is properly presented to it for judicial determination.

The facts of the *Ashwander* case afford a good insight into the intricacies of judicial government. Ashwander and other preferred stockholders protested to the board of directors of the Alabama Power Company that certain contracts concluded between the company and the Tennessee Valley Authority and its subsidiary, the Electric Home and Farm Authority, were invalid since they were beyond the constitutional power of the United States and injurious to corporate interests; and they de-

[58] Smith v. Kansas City Title Co. (1921), 255 U.S. 180, 201, 202.

manded that steps be taken to annul the contracts. The board refused to accede to this demand; and, afterwards, the Commonwealth and Southern Corporation, the holder of the common stock of the power company, refused to call a meeting of the stockholders to take action. Plaintiffs then brought suit to enjoin performance of the contracts and asked a general declaratory decree concerning the rights of the authority in its various relations. The United States District Court enjoined the performance of the contracts in a decree later reversed by the Circuit Court of Appeals of the Fifth Circuit.

Although the holdings of the plaintiffs' stock were small, about one-three hundred and fortieth of the preferred stock, Chief Justice Hughes, speaking for a concurring majority, ruled that the right to maintain the suit was not affected by the smallness of the holdings.[59] The requirement that litigants must stage a contest over substantial interests to get justice was thereby relaxed to permit them to fight over less substantial and more widely dispersed interests. Contrary to the principle of the holding in the later case of *Alabama Power Co. v. Ickes* [60] to the effect that a third party who suffered injuries from "the lawful use of unlawfully loaned" could not maintain a suit to enjoin the loan, the Court took the position that it was not necessary to show the transaction was *ultra vires* of the corporation, and that illegality might be found in lack of authority of those with whom the corporation was attempting to deal. In such a situation a stockholder could sue to prevent breach of duty

[59] Ashwander v. Tennessee Valley Authority (1936), 297 U.S. 288, 318.
[60] (1938), 302 U.S. 464.

by a corporation "in yielding, without appropriate resistance, to governmental demands which are without
warrant of law or are in violation of constitutional restrictions." [61]

Instead, however, of giving the information that every-
one, except parties fearful of an adverse decision, wanted
to know concerning the validity of the Tennessee Valley Authority, the Court, after finding an adversity of
parties, refused to take the equally easy additional step
of finding any other contested issue than that of the
power of the TVA to acquire transmission lines, thereby
leaving the validity of the activities of the TVA shrouded
in uncertainty for five years after the agency was created.
The Court, having thrown its own conception of a
"case" out of the window by the finding of adversity
of parties, brought it in through the door in other ways.

The sole issue, said the Court, was the validity of the
contract of January 4, 1934. All other issues were abstract or contingent. Hence this assertion: "The pro-
nouncements, policies, and program of the Tennessee
Valley Authority and its directors, their motives, and desires, did not give rise to a justiciable controversy save as
they had fruition in action of a definite and concrete
character constituting an actual or threatened interference with the rights of the persons complaining. The
judicial power does not extend to the determination of
abstract questions." [62] Since "assumed potential invasions
of rights are not enough to warrant judicial intervention," [63] the Court left the litigants to fight over other

---

[61] Ashwander v. Tennessee Valley Authority (1936), 297 U.S. 288,
319.

[62] Ibid., 324.   [63] Ibid., 324–325.

issues until the combat should pass beyond the stage of orderly dispute.

That "cases and controversies," "adverse parties," "substantial interests," and "real questions" are no more than trees behind which judges hide when they wish either to throw stones at Congress or the President or to escape from those who are urging them to do so is manifested by the contradictory attitude the Court took in *Alabama Power Co. v. Ickes.*[64] In this case bills were filed in a district court to enjoin Ickes and others from making WPA loans and grants to municipalities for the construction of municipally owned power distribution systems on the ground that such grants were unconstitutional and in any event beyond the purview of the statute. The petitioner alleged future loss of business as a result of competing distribution systems, and the District Court heard the case but denied the injunction on the merits of the case. The Circuit Court affirmed the decrees dismissing the bills but did so on the ground that no legal or equitable right had been invaded and that the petitioner had no standing in court to challenge the validity of the loans and grants.

The Supreme Court, too, could not find a sufficient interest in the financial loss of the company or in its interest as a taxpayer to give it a standing in court. With questions the Court responded to the litigants.

Can anyone who will suffer injurious consequences from the lawful use of money about to be unlawfully loaned maintain a suit to enjoin the loan? An affirmative answer would produce novel and startling results. And that question suggests another: Should the loan be consummated, may

[64] (1938), 302 U.S. 464.

such a one sue for damages? If so, upon what ground may he sue either the person making the loan, or the person receiving it? Considered apart, the lender owes the sufferer no enforcible duty to refrain from making the unauthorized loan; and the borrower owes him no obligation to refrain from using the proceeds in any lawful way the borrower may choose. If such a suit can be maintained, similar suits by innumerable persons are likewise admissible to determine whether money is being loaned without lawful authority for uses which, although hurtful to the complainants, are perfectly lawful. The supposition opens a vista of litigation hitherto unrevealed.[65]

Similar to the cases reviewed above are suits between states or those to which a state is a party. These cases involve attempts of states to protect their sovereign capacity against federal encroachment, actions brought by the states as *parens patriae*, and actions to protect the general interests of the states. Suits brought by states to protect their so-called sovereign rights and their existence as political entities have of one accord been dismissed.[66] The leading case is *Georgia v. Stanton*,[67] which was an original bill in equity brought by the state of Georgia against the Secretary of War, General Grant, and Major General Pope to restrain them from enforcing the Reconstruction Acts. Counsel for Georgia contended that the statement of the President affirming his intention to enforce the acts and the issuing of orders by General Grant for that purpose led to the presence of substantial fear, to quiet which a bill *quia timeat* was ap-

[65] *Ibid.*, 480–481.
[66] Georgia v. Stanton (1867), 6 Wall. 50; Mississippi v. Johnson (1867), 4 Wall. 475; Massachusetts v. Mellon (1923), 262 U.S. 447; New Jersey v. Sargent (1926), 269 U.S. 328.
[67] (1867), 6 Wall. 50.

propriate. Counsel argued further that the enforcement of the acts constituted "an immediate paralysis of all authority and power of the state government by military power" and "a proceeding to divest her of her legally and constitutionally established and guaranteed existence, as a body politic and a member of the Union." The Court dismissed the bill for want of jurisdiction over the subject matter on the ground that a case must be presented so as to be appropriate for the exercise of the judicial power because the rights threatened "must be rights of persons or property, not merely political rights, which do not belong to the jurisdiction of a court, either in law or equity." [68]

The rule laid down in *Georgia v. Stanton* was elaborated more than half a century later in *Massachusetts*

---

[68] *Ibid.*, 76. Speaking of the right of a state to exist as a corporate entity and the possibility of its government being overthrown and another substituted in its place, Justice Nelson said: "That these matters, both as stated in the body of the bill, and, in the prayers for relief, call for the judgment of the court upon political questions, and, upon rights, not of persons or property, but of a political character, will hardly be denied. For the rights for the protection of which our authority is invoked, are the rights of sovereignty, of political jurisdiction, of corporate existence as a state, with all its constitutional powers and privileges. No case of private rights of private property infringed, or in danger of actual or threatened infringement, is presented by the bill, in a judicial form, for the judgment of the court." P. 77. Cf. the dissenting opinion of Thompson, J. in Cherokee Nation v. Georgia (1831), 5 Pet. 1, 75, where he said: "It is only where the rights of persons or property are involved, and when such rights can be presented under some judicial form of proceedings, that courts of justice can interpose relief. This court can have no right to pronounce an abstract opinion upon the constitutionality of a state law. Such law must be brought into actual or threatened operation, upon rights properly falling under judicial cognizance, or a remedy is not to be had here." In the same case Chief Justice Marshall, speaking of the subject matter, said: "It savours too much of the exercise of political power to be within the proper province of the judicial department." P. 20.

v. Mellon.[69] This was a suit in equity brought by the state of Massachusetts in its own behalf and as *parens patriae* of taxpaying citizens to enjoin the enforcement of the Maternity Act, which, it was alleged, was a usurpation of the reserved rights of the state and an impairment of its sovereignty. The suit was dismissed for want of jurisdiction on the ground that a state could not maintain a suit either to protect its political rights or as *parens patriae* to protect citizens of the United States from the operation of the law thereof inasmuch as the proceeding was not a justiciable one and therefore without the contemplation of the grant of judicial power. Speaking of the right of the state to sue in its own behalf to protect its political rights, the Court reiterated the rule of *Georgia v. Stanton:*

> In that aspect of the case we are called upon to adjudicate, not rights of person or property, not rights of dominion over physical domain, not quasi-sovereign rights actually invaded or threatened, but abstract questions of political power, of sovereignty, of government. No rights of the State falling within the scope of the judicial power have been brought within the actual or threatened operation of the statute, and this Court is as much without authority to pass abstract opinions upon the constitutionality of acts of Congress as . . . of state statutes.[70]

New Jersey v. Sargent [71] is similar except that here the state alleged interference by the Federal Water Power Act with its conservation of potable waters, in-

[69] (1923), 262 U.S. 447.

[70] *Ibid.,* 484–485. See also Texas v. Interstate Commerce Commission (1922), 258 U.S. 158, 162. See, however, Penn. and Ohio v. W. Va. (1923), 262 U.S. 553, where some of the principles stated above were ignored.

[71] (1926), 269 U.S. 328.

jury to its reservoirs and waterworks, deprivation of revenue from submerged lands owned by the state in its sovereign capacity, interference with power projects contemplated by the state, and the imposition of onerous restrictions upon the state and its citizens. Because there was no showing of actual or threatened interference, the Court ruled that until the restrictions were given practical effect, the reserved rights of the state could not be made the subject of judicial inquiry. Accordingly, the sole purpose of the bill was to obtain a judicial declaration that certain sections of the act were void.[72] To the same effect is *Arizona v. California*,[73] where the Court in the exercise of its original jurisdiction refused to enjoin the Secretary of the Interior and the states of the Colorado River Compact from constructing Boulder Dam on the ground, among others, that the bill presented no case or controversy of which the Court could take judicial cognizance since no rights of Arizona were presently threatened and the Court could not issue declaratory decrees. For similar reasons the Court in *Alabama v. Arizona*[74] refused to enjoin five states from enforcing statutes prohibiting the open market sale of products of convict labor in spite of Alabama's investment of more than $300,000 in certain cotton mills. Any loss to the state from either a loss of markets or in increased cost of prison maintenance was a hypothetical question because Alabama might seek other markets.

The remaining suits to which a state was a party and which were dismissed as nonjusticiable present the emphasis on adversity of interest in a different aspect. Thus

[72] *Ibid.*, 339–340.   [73] (1931), 283 U.S. 423, 450.
[74] (1934), 291 U.S. 286.

it has been held that a state not engaged in the transportation of certain commodities did not have such interest in its corporate capacity as to enable it to maintain a suit to enjoin a railroad from charging more than a specified rate on domestic shipments.[75] Similarly a state does not have sufficient interest in the equitable administration of the quarantine laws of another state to enable it to invoke the original jurisdiction of the Supreme Court to restrain discrimination against its citizens and the obstruction of interstate commerce.[76] On the other hand, the interest of a state in the health of its citizens is sufficient to enable it to maintain a suit to enjoin the discharge of sewage into the Mississippi River,[77] as is the interest of a state sufficient to enjoin the protection of its forests and the purity of the air over its domain against the discharge of noxious gases by a manufacturing establishment in a bordering state.[78] A bill in equity is also "a reasonable and proper means to assert the alleged quasi-sovereign rights of a state" in the protection of wild game within the state as against federal encroachment upon the reserved rights of the state.[79]

The narrow definition which the term "cases and controversies" has come to possess is of signal importance in the application of the doctrine that courts cannot be charged with the performance of nonjudicial functions. Since the judicial power is limited to the decision of cases and controversies, any definition of this phrase which tends to expand or contract its scope produces a

[75] Oklahoma v. A. T. & S. F. R. Co. (1911), 220 U.S. 277.
[76] Louisiana v. Texas (1900), 176 U.S. 1.
[77] Missouri v. Illinois (1901), 180 U.S. 208, 243.
[78] Georgia v. Tennessee Copper Co. (1907), 206 U.S. 230, 237, 238.
[79] Missouri v. Holland (1920), 252 U.S. 416.

corresponding effect on the power of Congress to utilize the machinery of the courts in aid of administrative bodies, to charge the courts themselves with administrative duties, or to revise modes of procedure in the direction of providing for the declaratory judgment in the federal courts. As a matter of actual fact courts do perform nonjudicial functions and use their processes in aid of administrative agencies. They naturalize aliens,[80] use their power to punish for contempt to compel recalcitrant witnesses to obey the orders of administrative agencies,[81] and perform other duties of an administrative or executive nature;[82] but they do so only when such matters are presented to them in the form of a justiciable controversy. Hence, the utility of the federal courts as a branch of the broad scheme of government existing to advance its ends varies directly with the scope of the definition of the phrase "cases and controversies."

Turning first to the attitude of the courts towards the performance of nonjudicial functions when presented in a case or controversy, no instance is to be found in which the Supreme Court has refused to exercise jurisdiction because of the nonjudicial nature of the duties involved, although the lower federal courts have done so. In 1887 Congress created the Pacific Railway Commission to investigate the condition of railroads receiving aid from the federal government. The commission was empowered to require the attendance and testimony of witnesses; the circuit and district courts were authorized to issue or-

[80] Tutun v. U.S. (1926), 270 U.S. 568.
[81] I.C.C. v. Brimson (1894), 154 U.S. 447.
[82] See La Abra Silver Min. Co. v. U.S. (1899), 175 U.S. 423; Fong Yue Ting v. U.S. (1893), 149 U.S. 698; Old Colony Trust Company v. Commissioner of Internal Revenue (1929), 279 U.S. 716.

ders requiring witnesses to appear and testify, and failure to do so was made contempt of court. Leland Stanford of the Central Pacific Railroad refused to answer certain questions, whereupon the commission applied to a United States circuit court for an order compelling him to answer. This court, speaking through Justice Field, refused to grant the order on the grounds that the courts of the United States could not be made the instruments of the commission in furthering its investigation and that Congress could not require the exercise of the judicial power except in cases and controversies.[83]

Seven years later this decision was in effect overruled by the Supreme Court in *Interstate Commerce Commission v. Brimson*.[84] In pursuance of section 12 of the Interstate Commerce Act, the Interstate Commerce Commission applied for an order compelling the appearance and testimony of a witness. The Circuit Court regarded the proceeding as nonjudicial and as being merely in aid of an administrative body and refused to grant the order, although it admitted the proceeding would have been judicial had the statute provided for the prosecution of violations thereof.[85] In a labored opinion the Supreme Court reversed the action of the Circuit Court and ruled that the action was a case and, therefore, susceptible of judicial determination. Whether the commission was entitled to the evidence it was seeking and whether the refusal of the witness to testify and produce papers was in derogation of the rights of the United States were regarded as distinct issues which were so

[83] In re Pacific Ry. Comm. (C.C., N.D., Cal., 1887), 32 Fed. 241. See quotation from this case above.
[84] (1894), 154 U.S. 447.
[85] In re I.C.C. (C.C., N.D., Ill., 1892), 53 Fed. Rep. 476, 480.

presented as to render the judicial power capable of acting upon them.[86] The Court said:

The United States asserts its right under the Constitution and laws, to have these appellees answer the questions propounded to them by the Commission, and to produce specified books, papers, etc., in their possession or under their control. It insists that the evidence called for is material in the matter under investigation; that the subject of investigation is within legislative cognizance, and may be inquired of by any tribunal constituted by Congress for that purpose. The appellees deny that any such rights exist in the general government, or that they are under a legal duty, even if such evidence be important or vital in the enforcement of the Interstate Commerce Act, to do what is required of them by the Commission. Thus has arisen a dispute involving rights or claims asserted by the respective parties to it. And the power to determine it directly, and, as between the parties, finally, must reside somewhere. It cannot be that the general government, with all the power conferred upon it by the people of the United States, is helpless in such an emergency, and is unable to provide some method, judicial in form, and *direct in its operation*, for the prompt and conclusive determination of this dispute.[87]

Regarded in this way, the *Brimson* case simply holds that a proceeding is none the less judicial in nature because it has the effect of aiding an administrative agency. In other words, Congress cannot authorize courts of the United States to assist in the performance of administrative functions except through the vehicle of a case or

[86] (1894), 154 U.S. 447, 476–477.

[87] *Ibid.*, 477. As stated further by the Court: "The proceeding is one for determining rights arising out of specified matters in dispute that concern both the general public and the individual defendants. It is one in which a judgment may be rendered that will be conclusive upon the parties until reversed by this court, and that judgment may be enforced by the process of the Circuit Court." P. 487.

controversy in which the courts may render a final judgment.[88] The case of *Fong Yue Ting v. United States* [89] illustrates to a greater extent the difficulty of distinguishing between judicial and nonjudicial functions and the futility of attempting to draw a strict line of demarcation between executive and judicial power. An act of Congress of 1892 required the registration of Chinese subjects and made the lower federal courts direct administrative agencies for the expulsion of aliens unlawfully within the country and for the issuance of certificates to those entitled to remain. Moreover, it provided for a special procedure in such cases, and it prescribed what evidence should be received and the effect to be given such evidence.[90] Reviving the distinction made in *Murray v. Hoboken Land & Improvement Co.*[91] between matters involving public right which may be presented in such form that the judicial power is capable of acting upon them and which Congress may or may not withhold from judicial cognizance and those matters of private right which cannot be withdrawn from the judicial power, the Court went on to hold that the issues as pre-

---

[88] *Ibid.* Justice Brewer, with whom concurred Fuller, Ch.J., and Jackson, J., delivered a vigorous dissent in which he contended that no action was pending to enforce a right or redress a wrong. Such a power to authorize courts to use their process in aid of administrative bodies carried with it, he thought, "the power to make courts the mere assistants of every administrative board or executive officer, in the pursuit of any information desired or in the execution of any duties imposed." (1894), 155 U.S. 3, 4.

[89] (1893), 149 U.S. 698.

[90] For the acknowledged power of Congress to prescribe the evidence to be received and its effect in the courts of its own government, see Ogden v. Saunders (1827), 12 Wh. 213, 349, 362; Pillow v. Roberts (1852), 13 How. 472, 476; Cliquot's Champagne (1866), 3 Wall. 114, 143; Ex parte Fisk (1885), 113 U.S. 713, 721.

[91] (1856), 18 How. 272, 284.

sented constituted a case or controversy because "when in the form prescribed by law, the executive officer, acting in behalf of the United States, brings the Chinese laborer before the judge, in order that he may be heard, and the facts upon which depends his right to remain in the country be decided, a case is duly submitted to the judicial power; for here are all the elements of a civil case . . . a complainant, a defendant, and a judge . . . *actor, reus, et judix.* . . . No formal complaint or pleadings are required, and the want of them does not affect the authority of the judge, or the validity of the statute." [92]

To the same effect are *La Abra Silver Mining Co. v. United States* [93] and *Tutun v. United States.*[94] The former case involved the validity of an act of Congress which directed the Attorney General to bring a suit in the name of the United States against the appellants to determine whether an award made by an international claims commission, acting under a treaty between the United States and Mexico, was obtained by means of fraud. Full jurisdiction was conferred upon the Court of Claims, subject to appeal to the Supreme Court, to determine the suit, to make all the proper decrees therein, and to enforce the same by injunction. The Supreme Court sustained the validity of the act because the money received by the United States from Mexico was regarded as being in strict law the property of the United States, and because the interest of Congress in the honor of the government and the relations of this country with Mexico was sufficient to enable it to authorize a suit for

[92] (1893), 149 U.S. 698, 728–729.   [93] (1899), 175 U.S. 423.
[94] (1926), 270 U.S. 568.

the determination of a question "peculiarly judicial in nature." [95]

Even more significant is the *Tutun* case, where naturalization proceedings were held to constitute a case and therefore subject to review by the Circuit Court of Appeals. Justice Brandeis said, speaking for a unanimous court:

Whenever the law provides a remedy enforceable in the courts according to the regular course of legal procedure, and that remedy is pursued, there arises a case within the meaning of the Constitution, whether the subject of the litigation be property or status. A petition for naturalization is clearly a proceeding of that character.

The petitioner's claim is one arising under the Constitution and laws of the United States. The claim is presented to the court in such a form that the judicial power is capable of acting upon it. The proceeding is instituted and is conducted throughout according to the regular course of judicial procedure. The United States is always a possible adverse party. [96]

Accordingly, the award of a certificate of naturalization is a judicial judgment settling the rights of adverse parties.

In spite of the subtleties which lie concealed in the phrase "cases and controversies," awaiting discovery and revelation by judicial penetrations into the occult, these last cases demonstrate its flexibility and its capacity for expansion. In the light of these cases, the requirement of a case or controversy does not constitute so serious a limitation either to the exercise of judicial power or to

[95] 175 U.S. 423, 458–459.

[96] 270 U.S. 568, 577. This last is true because, it was argued, the statute preserves the rights of litigants to the United States.

legislative action relating to the jurisdiction and procedure of the lower federal courts. The limitation is largely one of judicial attitude. The courts have also emphasized the necessity of an actual controversy in cases in equity and especially in those where injunctive relief is sought against the enforcement of a statute alleged to be unconstitutional. Two reasons may be advanced for the attitude of the courts in this respect. In the first place, in order to prevent an abuse of their equity powers, the courts have thrown certain safeguards around equity. Second, certain types of injunctive relief bear a close resemblance to declaratory judgments of which the federal courts are a bit chary and from which they maintain a respectable distance. In any exercise of equity jurisdiction, therefore, there must be an actual wrong or threat of wrong and contested issues between adverse parties.

In accordance with this principle are the rules that the questions presented in such suits must be real and not academic or contingent and that such suits must not be prematurely brought.[97] In 1864 in *Cross v. Del Valle*,[98] the Supreme Court laid down the definite rule that the federal courts could not entertain a suit in equity to declare future rights. Justice Grier declared:

A chancellor will not maintain a bill *merely to declare future rights*. The Scotch tribunals pass on such questions by *"declarator,"* but the English courts have never assumed such power. . . . The court is not called upon to make a scheme of the trusts, nor could they anticipate the situation of the parties in the suit, or those who may be in existence at the death of Mrs. Del Valle. The court has no power to decree

[97] Turpin v. Lemon (1902), 187 U.S. 51, 61.
[98] (1864), 1 Wall. 1.

in thesi, as to the future rights of parties not before the court or *in esse.*[99]

In general the attitude of the courts toward the necessity of an actual controversy is much the same where injunctive relief is sought against statutes or administrative orders alleged to be unconstitutional as in cases where the validity of legislative or administrative acts are attacked in some manner. Thus an injunction will not lie against action by a state utilities commission before it has fixed rates because such is an attempt to enjoin legislation; [100] nor will an injunction lie to restrain the assessment of a tax on the stock and real estate of a national bank because of the apprehension that the assessing officer will violate the federal laws relating to the taxation of national banks.[101] As put by Justice Brandeis in another connection, "the fact that the plaintiff's desires are thwarted by its own doubts, or by the fear of others, does not confer a cause of action." [102]

In *Massachusetts State Grange v. Benton* [103] the Su-

[99] *Ibid.,* 14, 15, 16. The Supreme Court, as well as other courts, must deal with the case at hand and not speculate upon imaginary issues. Yazoo and Miss. V. R. Co. v. Jackson Vinegar Co. (1912), 226 U.S. 217, 219–220; Hatch v. Reardon (1907), 204 U.S. 152, 160; So. Ry. Co. v. King (1910), 217 U.S. 524, 534; Collins v. Texas (1912), 223 U.S. 288, 295; Standard Stock Food Co. v. Wright (1912), 225 U.S. 540, 550. That the English courts would not formerly declare future rights, see Grove v. Bastard, 2 Phil. 621, and Langdale v. Briggs, 39 Eng. L. & E. 214, to the effect that "the court does not declare future rights, but leaves them to be determined when they may come into possession." This was quoted in Cross v. Del Valle, 1 Wall. 1, 5. See also Sharon v. Tucker (1892), 144 U.S. 533, 543.

[100] McChord v. L. & N. R. Co. (1902), 183 U.S. 483. Cf. Prentis v. Atl. C. L. R. Co. (1908), 211 U.S. 210.

[101] First National Bank v. Albright (1908), 208 U.S. 548.

[102] Willing v. Chicago Auditorium Ass'n (1928), 277 U.S. 274, 289–290.

[103] (1926), 272 U.S. 525.

preme Court affirmed a decree dismissing a bill to restrain the execution of a daylight-saving act on the ground
that injunctions restrain state officials from enforcing a
state law only in cases "reasonably free from doubt and
when necessary to prevent great and irreparable injury";
but at the same time it sustained the jurisdiction of the
lower court to entertain the bill. Justice McReynolds in
a separate opinion contended that jurisdiction should not
have been exercised because the bill disclosed "a bold
purpose to secure an adjudication in respect of the constitutionality of a state statute. In no just sense did it seek
protection of any property right threatened with unlawful invasion by an officer claiming to proceed under a
void enactment." [104]

The distinction between what is a "bold attempt" to
secure the adjudication of the validity of a statute and a
justifiable resort to equity to prevent irreparable injury
to rights of persons or property is not easily drawn, but
in the vast majority of such cases the courts have manifested a tendency to entertain jurisdiction. The broad
definition of property in *International News Service v.
the Associated Press* [105] and other cases and the broad

---

[104] *Ibid.*, 529. For other cases in which the distinction between mere
attempt to secure an adjudication of the validity of a statute and a
bona fide case has been a bit tenuous and in which injunctive relief
resembles a declaration of rights, see Terrace v. Thompson (1923),
263 U.S. 197; Euclid v. Ambler Realty Co. (1926), 272 U.S. 365; Pierce
v. Society of Sisters (1925), 268 U.S. 510. The leading case on the use
of the injunction as an instrument for testing the validity of statutes
of states is Ex parte Young, 209 U.S. 123, decided in 1908.

[105] (1918), 248 U.S. 215, in which the Court affirmed a decree protecting a "property right" in "an uncopyrighted combination of
words" published as news. Among the rights of persons or property
protected by the due process clauses of the Fifth and Fourteenth
Amendments are the right to sell, lease, and dispose of land for a

view of what constitutes a wrong or threat of wrong
which the Court took in *Pennsylvania and Ohio v. West
Virginia* [106] have done much to remove the safeguards
thrown about equity and, therefore, to diminish the emphasis on the necessity of a case or controversy in injunction proceedings. In the latter case, especially, the
safeguards thrown about equity virtually disappear.

In 1919 the West Virginia legislature enacted a law
giving preference to local needs in the consumption of
natural gas and authorizing the public utilities commission to order companies having gas in excess of local
needs to supply to companies having an inadequate supply before shipping it from the state. Before the commission had acted, Pennsylvania and Ohio brought suits
to enjoin West Virginia from enforcing the act because
of the belief that its enforcement would largely curtail
or cut off the supply of natural gas going to those states
and would obstruct interstate commerce to the irreparable injury of public institutions using the gas, to the
jeopardy of the health and comfort of their citizens who
used the gas, and finally to the curtailment of many in-

lawful purpose (Terrace v. Thompson [1923], 263 U.S. 197); the
right to earn a livelihood and to continue in employment unmolested
(Truax v. Raich [1915], 239 U.S. 33); the right to follow a chosen
profession (Crane v. Johnson [1917], 242 U.S. 339); the right of ticket
scalpers to sell theater tickets at a rate of choice (Tyson & Bro. v.
Banton [1927], 273 U.S. 418); the right of public service corporations
to sell at a reasonable rate and that of others to sell at a rate of choice
(Van Dyke v. Geary [1917], 244 U.S. 39); the right to sell stocks,
bonds, or merchandise (Hall v. Geiger-Jones Co. [1917], 242 U.S.
539); the right of parents to send their children to private schools or
provide otherwise for their education (Pierce v. Society of Sisters
[1925], 268 U.S. 510).

[106] (1923), 262 U.S. 553.

dustries using reasonably large quantities of gas. In spite
of the fact that no action had been taken and that there
was nothing to indicate that the requirement for local
preference would diminish the supply sent to other states,
the Court held that the suits presented a direct issue between two states of the right of one to withdraw gas
from interstate commerce. Furthermore, the assertion
and denial that the withdrawal was an interference with
interstate commerce was regarded as "essentially a judicial question." "What is sought," said Justice Van Devanter, speaking for the majority, "is not an abstract ruling on that question, but an injunction against such a
withdrawal presently threatened and likely to be pro-
ductive of great injury. . . . The attitude of the complainant states is not that of mere volunteers attempting
to vindicate the freedom of interstate commerce or to
redress purely private grievances. Each sues to protect a
two-fold interest—one as the proprietor of various public
institutions and schools, whose supply of gas will be
largely curtailed or cut off by the threatened interference with the interstate current; and the other as the
representative of the consuming public whose supply
will be similarly affected. Both interests are substantial
and both are threatened with serious injury." [107] Speaking further of the interest of the state in the health, comfort, and welfare of private consumers, the Court continued: "This is a matter of grave public concern in
which the state, as the representative of the public, has
an interest apart from that of the individuals affected.
It is not merely a remote or ethical interest, but one

[107] *Ibid.*, 591.

which is immediate and which is recognized by law." [108]

To the contentions of the majority that the issues presented a justiciable controversy and that the suits were not prematurely brought, three of the judges dissented vigorously. In the view of Justice McReynolds the issues presented no justiciable controversy because the "vindication of the freedom of interstate commerce is not committed to any state as *parens patriae*." [109] Justice Brandeis was even more emphatic in contending that the proceedings did not constitute a case or controversy instituted according to the regular course of judicial procedure. "They are," he observed, ". . . an attempt to enjoin not executive action, but legislation. They are instituted frankly to secure from this court a general declaration that the West Virginia Act of February 17, 1919, is unconstitutional. . . . The mere enactment of the statute, obviously, does not constitute a threat to interrupt the flow of gas into the plaintiff states." [110]

---

[108] *Ibid.*, 592. Citing the following as being in point: Mo. v. Ill. (1901), 180 U.S. 208, 241; Kansas v. Colorado (1902), 185 U.S. 125, 141–143; Ga. v. Tenn. Copper Co. (1907), 206 U.S. 230, 237; N.Y. v. N.J. (1921), 256 U.S. 296, 301; and Wyoming v. Colo. (1922), 259 U.S. 419, 464. The following were cited as not being in point: N.H. v. La. (1883), 108 U.S. 76; La. v. Tex. (1900), 176 U.S. 1; Kansas v. U.S. (1907), 204 U.S. 331; Okla. v. A. T. & S. F. R. Co. (1911), 220 U.S. 277; and Tex. v. I.C.C. (1922), 258 U.S. 158, 162.

[109] (1923), 262 U.S. 553, 604.

[110] *Ibid.*, 610, 611. The dissent of Justice Brandeis is a good illustration of his belief in narrow judicial review and also of his conceptions of the limitations to judicial performance of administrative functions. On the latter point, referring to the inability of the Court to make an equitable distribution of natural gas, he said, "To make equitable distribution would be a task of such complexity and difficulty that even an interstate public service commission, with broad powers, perfected administrative machinery, ample resources, practical experience and no other duties, might fail to perform it satisfactorily. As this court would be powerless to frame a decree and

The total effect of the *International News Service* case and *Pennsylvania and Ohio v. West Virginia* was to vest in the federal judiciary a boundless discretion to create new rights and enforce them by injunction without the self-imposed limitation of an actual case or controversy. In equity at least the federal courts may issue a declaration of rights by means of an injunction which may be enforced by resort to the residual powers of the courts, or which, as in the latter case, may need no enforcement.

From the doctrine that the courts will not render advisory opinions or decide abstract questions not properly before them, it follows that courts will not determine moot cases or suits arranged by collusion between parties having no opposing interests. A moot case has been defined as "one which seeks to get a judgment on a pretended controversy, when in reality there is none, or a decision in advance about a right before it has been actually asserted and contested, or a judgment upon some matter which, when rendered, for any reason, cannot have any practical legal effect upon a then existing controversy." [111] A case may become moot because of a change in law, or in the status of the litigants, or because of some act of the parties which dissolves the controversy. [112]

---

provide machinery by means of which such equitable distribution of the available supply could be effected, it should, according to settled practice, refuse to entertain the suits." P. 623. Citing Rutland Marble Co. v. Ripley (1871), 10 Wall. 339, 358; Tex. and Pacific R. Co. v. Marshall (1890), 136 U.S. 393, 406; Giles v. Harris (1903), 189 U.S. 475, 487.

[111] Ex parte Steel (1908), 162 Fed. 694, 701.

[112] Lord v. Veazie (1850), 8 How. 251; Chamberlain v. Cleveland (1862), 1 Bl. 419; Wood Paper Co. v. Heft (1869), 8 Wall. 333; East

Courts do not sit as pathologists to conduct autopsies on dead issues. "The duty of this court, as of every other judicial tribunal," said Justice Gray in the leading case of *Mills v. Green*,[113] "is to decide actual controversies by a judgment which can be carried into effect, and not give opinions on moot questions or abstract propositions, or to declare principles or rules of law which cannot affect the matter at issue in the case before it."

Amicable actions on agreed cases, however, are to be distinguished from moot cases because they presuppose

Tenn., V. & G. R. Co. v. So. Tel. Co. (1888), 125 U.S. 695; South Spring Hill Gold Mining Co. v. Amador Medean Gold Mining Co. (1892), 145 U.S. 300; Dakota County v. Glidden (1885), 113 U.S. 222; San Mateo County v. So. Pac. R. Co. (1885), 116 U.S. 138; Little v. Bowers (1890), 134 U.S. 547; Calif. v. San Pablo & T. R. Co. (1893), 149 U.S. 308; Pennsylvania v. Wheeling & Belmont Bridge Co. (1851), 13 How. 518; (1856), 18 How. 421; U.S. v. Chambers (1934), 291 U.S. 217, wherein the Supreme Court sustained a decree of a district court dismissing prosecutions for violation of the prohibition laws for the lack of jurisdiction because of the subsequent repeal of the Eighteenth Amendment. For other cases dealing with mootness, see American Book Co. v. Kansas (1904), 193 U.S. 49; Jones v. Montague (1904), 194 U.S. 147; Williams v. Hagood (1878), 98 U.S. 72; U.S. v. Hamburg-American Co. (1916), 239 U.S. 466; Barker Painting Co. v. Local No. 734 (1930), 281 U.S. 462; Cincinnati v. Vester (1930), 281 U.S. 439; Blair v. U.S. (1919), 250 U.S. 273, 279; Richardson v. McChesney (1910), 218 U.S. 487; Hooker v. Burr (1904), 194 U.S. 415; Singer Mfg. Company v. Wright (1891), 141 U.S. 696; Mills v. Green (1895), 159 U.S. 651; Hatfield v. King (1902), 184 U.S. 162; Stearns v. Wood (1915), 236 U.S. 75.

[113] (1895), 159 U.S. 651, 653. This case was an appeal from a decree of the Circuit Court of Appeals dissolving an injunction restraining certain registration officials from performing acts which would exclude the appellant from the voting lists. The election in which appellant desired to vote was held prior to the appeal to the Supreme Court, thereby rendering the case moot. See also U.S. v. Evans (1909), 213 U.S. 297; Barker Painting Co. v. Local No. 734 (1930), 281 U.S. 462, 463-464; U.S. v. Hamburg-American Co. (1916), 239 U.S. 466, 475.

an actual dispute over real rights and adverse interests.[114] When these elements exist, the courts will take jurisdiction regardless of the fact that the action may be amicable or that it may have been brought upon an agreed state of facts.[115] Such actions must not be collusive, however.[116] The difficulty of maintaining a clear distinction between collusive actions and agreed cases is not always easily overcome as is shown by *Pollock v. Farmers' Loan and Trust Company* [117] and *Chicago and Grand Trunk R. Co. v. Wellman.*[118] In the former case a bill had been filed by a stockholder, on behalf of himself and others similarly situated, to restrain the trust company from paying income taxes under the Act of 1895. Attorney General Olney, with singular maladroitness, joined the government as a party to the suit instead of attacking it as collusive or of refraining from participation altogether, in which instance the government would not have been bound by the decision. The Court took jurisdiction without question even though the stockholder had no interest adverse to that of the corporation.[119] In the *Wellman* case, however, the Supreme Court refused to direct a writ of error to the Supreme Court of Michigan in a friendly suit for damages upon an agreed statement of facts on the ground that the courts could not be precluded from making an inquiry into the validity of

[114] Lord v. Veazie (1850), 8 How. 251, 255.

[115] Hylton v. U.S. (1796), 3 Dall. 171, a made case in which the Court did not even consider the question; Fletcher v. Peck (1810), 6 Cr. 87; Buchanan v. Warley (1917), 245 U.S. 60; Legal Tender Cases (1871), 12 Wall. 457.

[116] Lord v. Veazie (1850), 8 How. 251.

[117] (1895), 157 U.S. 429; 158 U.S. 601.   [118] (1892), 143 U.S. 339.

[119] Cf. Brushaber v. Union Pacific R. Co. (1916), 240 U.S. 1.

the act by an agreed statement of facts by the parties and that no appeal could lie immediately from the legislature to the courts.[120]

The obscurity surrounding the exercise of judicial power and the validity of legislative enactments relating thereto is by no means exhausted by these vague emanations from the judicial article. Other elements contribute to the prismatic effect produced by court construction of the judicial power. One of the most important of these is the requirement of judicial finality. Conclusiveness and finality of the interpretation of the standing law are the very essence of judicial power in the American system. Judicial finality is the major premise of which judicial review is the conclusion. The power to render a final decision binding upon the parties until reversed by a higher court, therefore, is a second prerequisite to the exercise of judicial power. But judges are apt to be "naïf, simple-minded men" and, therefore, susceptible to entanglement in the intricacies of a conceptualistic jurisprudence. This has happened frequently when judges have confused judicial finality with an award of execution.

To the apostolic Taney is due much, if not most, of the present confusion regarding the nature of the judicial power. Chief Justice Marshall, it has been seen, left to Congress a latitudinarian discretion in the definition of a case. Similarly, in *Wayman v. Southard* [121] he regarded the adoption of procedure and the formulation of rules for the guidance of courts as a legislative function within the plenary power of Congress; but, in holding that this function might be delegated to the courts, he assumed,

[120] (1892), 143 U.S. 339, 345–346.   [121] (1825), 10 Wh. 1.

in spite of the fiction that courts cannot perform non-judicial functions, that courts could exercise the delegated power to make rules governing final process. Marshall employed the judicial power to exalt national supremacy. The result of his labors was to increase congressional authority. Taney, on the other hand, regarded the national judiciary not as an active force in the administration of the affairs of the national government, but as something of an autonomous unit designed for the purpose of preserving a nice equilibrium between the centripetal and centrifugal forces in the federal system. Accordingly, he exalted judicial power at the expense of congressional authority.

To be sure, Taney did not initiate the exaltation of judicial power. As early as 1792 the circuit courts for the districts of New York, Pennsylvania, and North Carolina refused to administer an act of Congress relating to invalid pensions because the action of the courts upon applications for pensions was made subject to revision by Congress and the Secretary of War.[122] The judges were of one accord in the belief that the duties required

[122] For the correspondence of the judges in which they gave their reasons for refusing the execution of the act, see Frankfurter and Davison, *Cases on Administrative Law*, 202–205, n. 6. In the same year a motion for mandamus was filed in the Supreme Court of the United States to direct the Circuit Court for the District of Pennsylvania to proceed in a petition of William Hayburn, who had applied for a pension. The Court held the motion under advisement until the next term, but when the Court reconvened Congress had amended the earlier law by the Act of February 28, 1793. Hayburn's Case (1792), 2 Dall. 409. The composition of the circuit courts renders certain what the decision of the Supreme Court would have been had it passed on the question. Chief Justice Jay and Justice Cushing were members of the Circuit Court for the District of New York; Justices Wilson and Blair in Pennsylvania; and Justice Iredell in North Carolina.

by the act were nonjudicial in nature and could not be performed by the courts. The judges of the Circuit Court for New York consented to perform the functions pre-scribed by the act in the capacity of commissioners; the judges for the Pennsylvania circuit refused to act at all; and those for the North Carolina circuit wrote their sentiments to President Washington in what is the only strictly advisory opinion in the history of the federal judiciary.[123]

One year later the Court, with polite but persistent obstinacy, refused to grant the request of the President and his Secretary of State to construe the treaties and laws of the United States in so far as they related to the questions arising out of the wars of the French Revolu-tion.[124] In 1794 the Supreme Court decided a case aris-ing under the Pension Act of 1792. Although the case is

[123] The language of Justice Iredell and Judge Sitgreaves, of the North Carolina circuit, is interesting: "No application has yet been made to the court, or to ourselves individually, and therefore we have had some doubts as to the propriety of giving an opinion in a case which has not yet come regularly and judicially before us. None can be more sensible than we are of the necessity of judges being in general extremely cautious in not intimating an opinion in any case extra-judicially, because we well know how liable the best minds are, not-withstanding their utmost care, to a bias, which may arise from a pre-conceived opinion, even unguardedly, much more deliberately given. But in the present instance, as many unfortunate and meritorious in-dividuals, whom Congress have justly thought proper subjects of immediate relief, may suffer great distress even by a short delay, and may be utterly ruined by a long one, we determined at all events to make our sentiments known as early as possible, considering this as a case which must be deemed an exception to the general rule, upon every principle of humanity and justice; resolving, however, that so far as we are concerned, individually, in case an application should be made, we will most attentively hear it. . . ." Frankfurter and Davison, op. cit., 205.

[124] Charles Warren, *The Supreme Court in United States History* (2nd ed.), I, 69 ff.

not reported, evidence later discovered purports to show that the Court sustained the Circuit Court's view that the power conferred on the courts was not judicial and that the judges could not exercise the power out of courts as commissioners.[125]

[125] U.S. v. Yale Todd. The note was inserted by Chief Justice Taney upon order of the Court in U.S. v. Ferreira (1851), 13 How. 40–52. Actually, of course, the Supreme Court renders advisory opinions in a variety of ways. After the Court had refused to render an advisory opinion to the executive upon the request of Jefferson who was then Secretary of State, it rendered one when President Monroe asked the judges for legal advice on the power of the government to appropriate federal funds for public improvements. The judges answered that Congress might do so under the war and postal powers. Professor Albertsworth has demonstrated that the Court or its individual members perform advisory functions under various labels. He has found the Court exercising advisory functions in giving counsel and advice to Congress and its committees on legislation pertaining to the judiciary, in the advisory nature of judicial dissents, in obiter dicta advisory to congressional or state action, and in judicial construction to compel congressional or state action. E. F. Albertsworth, "Advisory Functions in Federal Supreme Court" (1935), 23 Georgetown L. Journal 643, 644–647.

One of the most amazing advisory opinions of the members of the Court is the gratuitous opinion of Chief Justice Hughes in a letter to Senator Wheeler concerning Professor Corwin's proposal that the Court sit in divisions. Speaking of such a plan, the Chief Justice said: "It is believed that such a plan would be impracticable. A large proportion of the cases we hear are important and a decision by a part of the Court would be unsatisfactory. I may also call attention to the provisions of Article III, section 1, of the Constitution that the judicial power of the United States shall be vested 'in one Supreme Court' and in such inferior courts as the Congress may from time to time ordain and establish. The Constitution does not appear to authorize two or more Supreme Courts or two or more parts of a supreme court functioning in effect as separate courts." Reorganization of the Federal Judiciary, Hearings on S. 1392; 75th Congress, 1st Session, 1937, Pt. 3, p. 491. The letter is all the more amazing in that no restrictions were put on Senator Wheeler's use of it. He read it before the Judiciary Committee of the Senate on March 22, 1937, the day after it was written. In addition to this advice the Chief Justice also disputed the Attorney General's assertions concerning the Court's ability to clear

Upon this foundation Taney began his work on the elevation of the judicial power in *United States v. Ferreira*.[126] This case involved the validity of an act of Congress which directed the judge of the territorial court of Florida to examine and adjudge certain claims of Spanish subjects against the United States and to report his decisions and evidence thereon to the Secretary of the Treasury who, upon being satisfied that the decisions were just and within the treaty, was to pay the amount of the award to the claimant. In 1849, after Florida had become a state and the territorial court a district court of the United States, the Supreme Court refused to hear an appeal brought by the United States for want of jurisdiction. The only difference between this act and the Act of 1792, it was pointed out, was that the former was directed to the judge individually whereas the latter was directed to the courts as such. Accordingly, the judge constituted a special tribunal whose authority was that of a commission to make an award and not that of a court of the United States to render a judicial decision. Although the power conferred upon the judges and the Secretary of the Treasury was judicial in nature in so far as it involved the exercise of judgment and discretion, it was not judicial power "in the sense in which judicial power is granted by the Constitution to the courts of the United States." [127] The Chief Justice might have stopped

its docket. Justices Van Devanter and Brandeis approved the letter. For Professor Corwin's explanation of his plan before the Senate Committee on the Judiciary see Reorganization of the Federal Judiciary, Hearings on S. 1392; 75th Congress, 1st Session, 1937, Pt. 2, pp. 172–173, 178, 179, 183, 202.

[126] (1851), 13 How. 40.

[127] *Ibid.*, 48. Commenting on the procedure prescribed by the act and its nonjudicial aspects, the Chief Justice said: "For there is to be

here, but he went on to raise the question of whether the commissioners appointed to adjust the claims were officers of the United States requiring appointment by the President and confirmation by the Senate. The question did not arise in the case and was not decided, but it afforded the Chief Justice the opportunity of remarking that "the duties to be performed are entirely alien to the legitimate functions of a judge or court of justice, and have no analogy to the general or special powers ordinarily and legally conferred on judges or courts to secure the due administration of the laws." [128]

Though Taney did little more here than formulate the results of *Hayburn's Case* and *United States v. Yale Todd* in an authenticated judicial opinion, he dropped intimations which anticipated future decisions. In indicating that under the act no process could issue and that no transcript of a record existed which the Supreme Court could regard as evidence of a proceeding or judgment in the lower court, he implied that such were necessary. In his opinion in *Gordon v. United States* [129] and in subsequent decisions accepting its doctrines, the intimation that an award of execution was a necessary element in the exercise of the judicial power became an accom-

---

no suit; no parties in the legal acceptance of the term, are to be made—no process to issue; and no one is authorized to appear on behalf of the United States, or to summon witnesses in the case. The proceeding is altogether ex parte; and all that the judge is required to do is to receive the claim where the party presents it, and to adjust it upon such evidence as he may have before him, or be able himself to obtain." P. 46.

[128] *Ibid.*, 51.

[129] (1865), 2 Wall. 561; 117 U.S. 697. No formal opinion of the Court was ever delivered in this important case. Chief Justice Taney prepared an opinion, but before the Court reconvened he died. His opinion was later published in 117 U.S. 697.

plished fact. A careful study of this case and of Taney's opinion is, therefore, necessary.

The act creating the Court of Claims provided for an appeal to the Supreme Court in certain cases after which final judgments in favor of claimants were to be referred to the Secretary of the Treasury, who should pay money out of any general appropriation made for the payment of private claims. Section 14 of the act, however, provided that no money should be paid out of the treasury "for any claim . . . till after an appropriation therefor shall be estimated for by the Secretary of the Treasury." The execution of the judgments of the Court of Claims and the Supreme Court in such cases depended, therefore, upon further action by the Secretary of the Treasury and Congress. When the first appeal came to the Supreme Court under the act, a majority of the judges concluded that the Court, under the Constitution, could exercise no appellate jurisdiction over the Court of Claims. Justice Miller and Justice Field dissented, but neither the majority nor the minority announced the reasons for its conclusion.

Whether Taney's opinion in *Gordon v. United States* was the basis of the decision of the Court is a matter of conjecture, but subsequent reiteration of it by the Court made much of it good law. Because the judgment of the Court of Claims and the Supreme Court depended for its execution upon future action of the Secretary of the Treasury and of Congress, Taney regarded it as nothing more than a certificate of opinion to the Secretary and not in any sense a judicial judgment.[130] Congress, therefore, could not authorize the Supreme Court to take ap-

130 *Ibid.*, 698–699.

peals from an auditor or require it to express an opinion on a case where its judicial power could not be exercised, and where its judgments would not be final and conclusive upon the parties, and where processes of execution were not awarded to carry it into effect. "The award of execution," he continued, "is a part and an essential part of every judgment passed by a court exercising judicial powers. It is no judgment in the legal sense of the term without it. Without such an award, the judgment would be inoperative and nugatory, leaving the aggrieved party without a remedy. . . . Such is not the judicial power confided in this court, in the exercise of its appellate jurisdiction." [131]

Taney's confusion of finality of judgment and the necessity of an award of execution were incorporated by the Court into many decisions with the result that the power of the courts to render such an award became one of the criteria of the judicial power.[132] Although that part of the opinion holding that the Supreme Court can only hear appeals on final judgments is still good law,[133]

---

[131] *Ibid.*, 702. See also on this point, Hunt v. Palao (1846), 4 How. 589; McNulty v. Batty (1850), 10 How. 72, 79.

[132] In re Sanborn (1893), 148 U.S. 222, 226; Frasch v. Moore (1908), 211 U.S. 1; Muskrat v. U.S. (1911), 219 U.S. 346, 355, 361-362; La Abra Silver Min. Co. v. U.S. (1899), 175 U.S. 423, 457; I.C.C. v. Brimson (1894), 154 U.S. 447, 483; Postum Cereal Co. v. Cal. Fig Nut Co. (1927), 272 U.S. 693.

[133] Fidelity Nat. Bk. v. Swope (1927), 274 U.S. 123; N., C., & St. L. R. Co. v. Wallace (1933), 288 U.S. 249; Virginia v. West Virginia (1918), 246 U.S. 565. For adjudication of boundary disputes where no award of execution has issued, see La. v. Miss. (1906), 202 U.S. 1; Ark. v. Tenn. (1918), 246 U.S. 158; Ga. v. S.C. (1922), 257 U.S. 516; Okla. v. Tex. (1926), 272 U.S. 21; Mich. v. Wis. (1926), 272 U.S. 398. The Supreme Court has also reviewed judgments of the Court of Claims though no process issued against the government. U.S. v. Jones (1886), 119 U.S. 477; D.C. v. Eslin (1901), 183 U.S. 62; Ex parte

it is no longer true that an award of execution is an essential element in the exercise of the judicial power.

Not until 1927 did the Court definitely dispose of the rule that an award of execution was an essential part of every judgment. In *Fidelity National Bank v. Swope* [134] was involved the power of the Supreme Court to hear an appeal under a city ordinance which directed that suits be brought by the city against property owners for the purpose of determining the validity of the ordinance and certain liens made under it for improvements. No appeal was taken from the decree of the state court upholding the ordinance and the liens which therefore became final. A suit was subsequently brought in a United States district court to annul the ordinance and cancel the liens. Unlike the actions in the *Muskrat* and *Gordon* cases, the proceeding was regarded as a judicial proceeding in which the judgment of the state court was *res judicata* and binding upon the parties until reversed on appeal. The reasoning of the Court is important. Since the issues, if raised in a suit by the taxpayer to enjoin collection of the assessment, would constitute a case or controversy, they could not, said Justice Stone, "be deemed any the less so, because through a modified procedure the parties are reversed and the same issues are raised and finally determined at the behest of the city." [135] Thus the difficulties of the *Muskrat* case are overcome.

The *Gordon* case is disposed of with similar ease.

Pocono Pines Hotel Co. (1932), 285 U.S. 526. See also Tutun v. U.S. (1926), 270 U.S. 568; and Old Colony Trust Co. v. Commissioner of Internal Revenue (1929), 279 U.S. 716.

[134] (1927), 274 U.S. 123.   [135] *Ibid.*, 131.

"While ordinarily," said the Court, "a case or judicial controversy results in a judgment requiring award of process of execution to carry it into effect, such relief is not an indispensable adjunct to the exercise of the judicial function." [136] Naturalization proceedings,[137] suits to determine matrimonial or other status or for instructions to a trustee or for the construction of wills,[138] bills of interpleader in so far as the stockholder is concerned,[139] and bills to quiet title where the plaintiff rests his claim on adverse possession were all cited as examples of cases where a writ of execution was not necessary to carry a judgment into effect.[140]

The holding that consequential relief is not a necessary adjunct of the exercise of judicial power does much to rescue the judicial article from the confusion into which Chief Justice Taney plunged it. It is still true, however, that the Supreme Court can review only final and judicial judgments,[141] that is, judgments which bind the parties in a "case" in the sense that the term is used in

---

[136] *Ibid.*, 132.   [137] Tutun v. U.S. (1926), 270 U.S. 568.

[138] Traphagen v. Levy (1889), 45 N.J. Eq. 448; 18 Atl. 222.

[139] Wakeman v. Kingsland (1889), 46 N.J. Eq. 113; 18 Atl. 680.

[140] Sharon v. Tucker (1892), 144 U.S. 533. Commenting further upon the issues and the subject matter presented, the Court said: "There is no want of adverse parties necessary to the creation of a controversy. . . . It [the judgment] operates to determine judicially the legal limits of the benefit district and to define rights of the parties in lands specifically described in the pleadings. So far as it affects owners of land in the benefit district who are citizens of other states, the controversy is a 'suit' which may be removed to the federal courts." 274 U.S. 123, 134.

[141] Federal Radio Commission v. General Electric Co. (1930), 281 U.S. 464, 469; Keller v. Potomac Electric Power Co. (1923), 261 U.S. 428; Postum Cereal Co. v. Cal. Fig Nut Co. (1927), 272 U.S. 693; In re Sanborn (1893), 148 U.S. 222; Frasch v. Moore (1908), 211 U.S. 1; B. & O. R.R. Co. v. I.C.C. (1909), 215 U.S. 216.

Article III.[142] Accordingly, the tenuous distinctions associated with the phrase "cases and controversies" remain. Then, too, there is no clear and precise conception of the term "final judgment," and Taney's ghost still walks.[143]

The general rule that the federal judiciary will not render advisory opinions, or perform nonjudicial functions, or decide other than actual cases or controversies involving real issues between adverse litigants has produced at times wholly unwarranted results. Thus the refusal of the courts in *Cross v. Del Valle* [144] to entertain a bill in equity because its sole purpose was to secure a declaration of private rights of a contingent nature without authorization of statute evolved into a temporary refusal of the federal judiciary to conform to the declaratory judgment acts of the states and created serious doubts concerning the power of Congress to enact a declaratory judgment statute.

The nature and purposes of the declaratory judgment have been treated in detail elsewhere.[145] Suffice it to

[142] Postum Cereal Co. v. Cal. Fig Nut Co. (1927), 272 U.S. 693, 698–699.

[143] Old Colony Trust Co. v. Commissioner of Internal Revenue (1929), 279 U.S. 716. For a proceeding to be judicial, said the Court, "it is enough that before the judgment which must be final has been invoked as an exercise of judicial power, it [the proceeding] shall have certain necessary features." For this case the necessary features were adverse parties and finality of judgment. Pp. 723–724. See also Federal Radio Commission v. General Electric Co. (1923), 261 U.S. 428; Butterworth v. U.S. ex rel. Hoe (1884), 112 U.S. 50, 60; U.S. v. Duell (1899), 172 U.S. 576; Baldwin Co. v. R. S. Howard Co. (1921), 256 U.S. 35.

[144] (1864), 1 Wall. 1.

[145] Edson R. Sunderland, "A Modern Evolution in Remedial Rights —the Declaratory Judgment" (1917), 16 Mich. L. Rev. 69; "The Courts as Authorized Legal Advisors of the People" (1920), 54 Am. L. Rev.

say that the declaratory judgment is a procedural reform aimed at securing remedial justice and the means
whereby a party, in order to terminate uncertainty, may
obtain from the courts a declaration of his rights, duties,
or status under the law or legal instruments before any
rights have actually been infringed or duties violated
and regardless of whether consequential relief may be
granted. At present the United States and more than
thirty states and territories have declaratory judgment
statutes, all of which, with the exception of the first
Michigan statute, have been upheld when their validity
was contested.[146] In general these statutes confer upon

161; Edwin M. Borchard, "The Constitutionality of Declaratory Judg-
ment in Federal Courts" (1932), 41 Yale L. Journal 1195; "Declaratory
Judgments in Pennsylvania" (1934), 82 Univ. of Penn. L. Rev. 317;
Declaratory Judgments (Cleveland, 1934). See also "Judicial Relief for
Peril and Insecurity" (1932), 45 Harv. L. Rev. 793, and the following
notes: "Declaratory Relief in the Supreme Court" (1932), 45 Harv.
L. Rev. 1089; "Constitutionality of the Declaratory Judgment Act as
Affected by the Scope of Judicial Functions" (1925), 11 Va. L. Rev.
473; "Courts and Procedure—Jurisdiction over Declaratory Judgments"
(1927), 13 Va. L. Rev. 644. For the attitude of the English courts
toward the declaratory judgment, see W. Ivor Jennings, "Declaratory
Judgments against Public Authorities in England" (1932), 41 Yale L.
Journal 407.

[146] For state cases upholding declaratory judgment statutes, see
Morton v. Pacific Const. Co. (1929), 36 Ariz. 97; 283 Pac. 281; Blakes-
lee v. Wilson (1923), 190 Cal. 479; 213 Pac. 495; Braman v. Babcock
(1923), 98 Conn. 549; 120 Atl. 150; Sheldon v. Powell (1930), 99 Fla.
782; 128 So. 258; Zoercher v. Agler (1930), 202 Ind. 214; 172 N.E. 186;
State ex rel. Hopkins v. Grove (1921), 109 Kan. 619; 201 Pac. 82;
Black v. Elkhorn Coal Corp. (1930), 233 Ky. 588; 26 S.W. (2nd) 481;
Washington-Detroit Theatre Co. v. Moore (1930), 249 Mich. 673;
229 N.W. 618; Lynn v. Kearney County (1931), 121 Neb. 122; 236
N.W. 192; Faulkner v. City of Keene (1931), 85 N.H. 147; 155 Atl.
195; McCrory Stores Corp. v. S. M. Braunstein (1926), 102 N.J. 590;
134 Atl. 752; Bd. of Educ. v. Van Zandt (1923), 119 Misc. 124; 195
N.Y.S. 297; Aff'd (1925), 234 N.Y. 644; 138 N.E. 481; Miller v. Miller
(1924), 149 Tenn. 463; 261 S.W. 965; Patterson's Ex'rs v. Patterson

courts of record within their respective jurisdictions the power to declare rights, status, and other legal relations of any interested parties "in cases of actual controversy" regardless of further relief as the affirmative or negative nature of the decree. Further relief may be granted if necessary, and courts may refuse to make a declaration where it would not terminate the uncertainty giving rise to the proceeding. Such judgments, when issued, have the same force and effect as any other final judgment [147] and are *res judicata* upon the parties. As construed by the state courts, declaratory judgment statutes require the existence of real issues and substantial interests between the adverse litigants. The courts will not determine abstract or hypothetical questions and will exercise jurisdiction in declaratory proceedings only when satisfied that "an actual controversy, or the ripening seeds of one, exists between parties all of whom are *sui juris* and before the court." [148]

(1926), 144 Va. 133; 131 S.E. 217; City of Milwaukee v. Chic. & N.W. Ry. Co. (1930), 201 Wis. 512; 230 N.W. 626; Holly Sugar Co. v. Fritzler (1931), 42 Wyo. 446; 296 Pac. 206. The validity of declaratory judgment acts has been assumed in other states. For an early reversal of a declaratory judgment statute, see Anway v. Grand Rapids Ry. Co. (1920), 211 Mich. 592; 179 N.W. 350.

[147] See the articles by Borchard, *supra*.

[148] Kariher's Petition (1925), 284 Penn. 455, 471; 131 Atl. 265, 271; Borchard, "Declaratory Judgments in Pennsylvania"; Williams v. Flood (1928), 124 Kan. 728; 262 Pac. 563; In re Cryan's Estate (1930), 301 Penn. 386; 152 Atl. 675; Hess v. Country Club Park, 296 Pac. 300 (Cal. App., 1931); Kelly v. Jackson (1925), 206 Ky. 815; 268 S.W. 539; Perry v. City of Elizabethton (1929), 160 Tenn. 102; 22 S.W. (2nd) 359; Fox v. Title & Trust Co. (1929), 129 Ore. 530; 277 Pac. 1003. See also the cases cited in 12 A.L.R. 52, 19 A.L.R. 1124, 50 A.L.R. 42.

Speaking of the necessity of an actual controversy, the Pennsylvania Supreme Court said: "Moreover, in a declaratory judgment proceeding the court will not decide future rights in anticipation of an event which may not happen, but, just as in the ordinary executory

In view of the fact that the United States and more than half of the states are now using the declaratory judgment, the attitude of the federal courts is important. Obviously, the past refusal of federal courts to use the new procedure and that of the Supreme Court to hear appeals from the declaratory judgment did much to impair its efficacy as an instrument of preventive justice. What the attitude of the federal judiciary would be was doubtful until 1927 when the Supreme Court ruled that the lower federal courts could not entertain a petition for a declaratory judgment under the conformity act because such a proceeding was not a case or controversy.[149] One year later, in line with this ruling, the Court ruled that it could exercise no appellate jurisdiction in decla-

---

action, it will wait until the event actually takes place, unless special circumstances appear which warrant an immediate decision, as for instance, where present rights depend on the declaration sought by plaintiff; and even then such rights will not be determined unless all parties concerned in their adjudication are present and ready to proceed with the case . . . so that the judgment rendered will make the issues involved res judicata in the full sense of that term." Kariher's Petition, 284 Penn. 455, 471; 131 Atl. 265, 271; citing In re Staples (1916), 1 Ch. 322; Norton v. Moren (1924), 206 Ky. 415; 267 S.W. 171; Ackerman v. Union & N.H. Tr. (1917), 91 Conn. 500; 100 Atl. 22. Cf. Lewis v. Green (1905), 2 Ch. 340; State v. Bd. of Comm'rs (1924), 117 Kan. 151; 230 Pac. 531; Axton v. Goodman (1924), 205 Ky. 382; 265 S.W. 806; Ezzell v. Exall (1925), 207 Ky. 615; 269 S.W. 752. To the same effect the Supreme Court of Tennessee said in Miller v. Miller (1924), 149 Tenn. 463, 487; 261 S.W. 965, 972: "It follows, therefore . . . that the only controversy necessary to invoke the action of the court and have it to declare rights under our declaratory judgment statute is that the question must be real and not theoretical; the person raising it must have a real interest, and there must be some one having a real interest in the question who may oppose the declaration sought. It is not necessary that any breach should be first committed, any right invaded, or wrong done." In this case there was no present actual controversy in the sense of threatened litigation.

[149] Liberty Warehouse Co. v. Grannis (1927), 273 U.S. 70; Willing v. Chicago Auditorium Ass'n (1928), 277 U.S. 274.

ratory judgment proceedings.[150] In February, 1933, however, the Supreme Court modified these rulings by holding that it would hear appeals from declaratory judgments in cases where an injunction might issue.[151] In 1934 Congress enacted the federal declaratory judgment statute which vests the federal courts with power "to declare rights and other legal relations of any interested party" in "cases of actual controversy" upon appropriate pleadings.

Equipped as it is with such neat juristic handles as "interested party" and "cases of actual controversy," the declaratory judgment may be turned to almost any purpose by the courts in their application of it. Hence the jargon of the Court in the past concerning the meaning of "case" and its fluctuating attitudes toward the declaratory judgment are more than likely to limit the effectiveness of this relatively new procedural device as an instrument of preventive justice.

The positions of the Court in these cases are difficult to reconcile and deserve close examination. In the *Grannis* case plaintiffs sought to obtain a declaration of rights in a United States district court under an act of 1924 regulating sales of leaf tobacco at public auction, which they contended was invalid as a violation of the commerce and due process clauses of the Federal Constitution. Plaintiffs alleged the existence of an actual controversy and threats of criminal and civil punishment in case of violation. That injunction proceedings on a simi-

---

[150] Liberty Warehouse Co. v. Burley Tobacco Growers' Association (1928), 276 U.S. 71.
[151] N., C., & St. L. R. Co. v. Wallace, 288 U.S. 249.

lar state of facts would have been entertained is evident from a perusal of injunction suits to restrain the enforcement of statutes alleged to be unconstitutional, but in this instance the District Court dismissed the petition for want of jurisdiction. The Supreme Court sustained the District Court on the ground of previously established principles concerning the nature of a case or controversy.[152]

The *Willing* case presented a far different situation from that presented by the *Grannis* case. Here certain lessors had failed to admit the right of the lessee company to tear down a building and replace it by a better one. In the course of what was designated as "an informal, friendly, private conversation," one of the lessors informed the president of the auditorium association that his counsel had advised him that the lessee had no right to demolish the building without the consent of the lessors. The association then instituted a suit to remove the cloud on the title to the leasehold. The bill alleged that "claims, fears, and uncertainties respecting the rights of the parties" to the leases greatly impaired their value and were clouds upon the title against which the association had no adequate remedy at law. Because there was no showing that defendants had hampered the full use of the premises, there was neither a hostile act nor a threat; the Supreme Court sustained the decree of the lower tribunal dismissing the bill on the ground

[152] (1927), 273 U.S. 70, 74. Citing Fairchild v. Hughes (1922), 258 U.S. 126; Muskrat v. U.S. (1911), 219 U.S. 346; Texas v. I.C.C. (1922), 258 U.S. 158; Keller v. Potomac Electric Power Co. (1923), 261 U.S. 428; Mass. v. Mellon (1923), 262 U.S. 447; N.J. v. Sargent (1926), 269 U.S. 328; Postum Cereal Co. v. Cal. Fig Nut Co. (1927), 272 U.S. 693.

that the plaintiff was seeking a mere declaratory judgment.[153]

Although it was true that the proceeding was not a moot case [154] or an administrative proceeding,[155] that a final judgment might have been rendered,[156] that there were adverse parties,[157] that plaintiff had a substantial interest in the question,[158] that the alleged interest was "definite and specific," [159] and that there was no attempt to obtain an abstract determination from the court,[160] still, the proceeding was not a case or controversy. That the plaintiff's desires were "thwarted by its own doubts, or by the fears of others," was not sufficient to confer a cause of action.[161]

Previously, in 1927, the Supreme Court had ruled in *Fidelity National Bank v. Swope* [162] that an award of execution was not an indispensable adjunct to the judicial process and made general statements which went

[153] (1928), 277 U.S. 274, 288–289.
[154] Singer Mfg. Co. v. Wright (1891), 141 U.S. 696; U.S. v. Alaska S.S. Co. (1920), 253 U.S. 113.
[155] Keller v. Potomac Electric Power Co. (1923), 261 U.S. 428; Postum Cereal Co. v. Cal. Fig Nut Co. (1927), 272 U.S. 693.
[156] Gordon v. U.S. (1864), 117 U.S. 697.
[157] South Spring Hill Gold Mining Co. v. Amador Medean Gold Mining Co. (1892), 145 U.S. 300.
[158] Fairchild v. Hughes (1922), 258 U.S. 126; Mass. v. Mellon (1923), 262 U.S. 447.
[159] N.J. v. Sargent (1926), 269 U.S. 328.
[160] Muskrat v. U.S. (1911), 219 U.S. 346; Texas v. I.C.C. (1922), 258 U.S. 158.
[161] (1928), 277 U.S. 274, 289–290. Justice Stone's concluding sentence in his concurring opinion deserves quotation. "And the determination now made seems to me very similar itself to a declaratory judgment to the effect that we could not constitutionally be authorized to give such judgments—but is in addition prospective, unasked, and unauthorized under any statute." *Ibid.*, 290, 291.
[162] 274 U.S. 123.

far in refuting some of the results in the *Grannis* and *Willing* cases. It regarded a modified form of proceeding as judicial in nature and ruled that an award of execution was not an essential of a judicial proceeding. Because the issues, had they been raised by a taxpayer in a suit to enjoin collection, would have constituted a case or controversy, they could not, in the view of Justice Stone, "be deemed any the less so because through a modified procedure the parties are reversed and the same issues are raised and finally determined at the behest of the city." [163]

Although the Court recognized that the effect of a city ordinance was to authorize the state court to examine and determine the validity and effect of legislative action and that the result of the proceeding was judicially to establish the validity of certain assessments, it held that the issues were so presented that the judicial power was capable of acting upon them. There was "no want of adverse parties necessary to the creation of a controversy" nor was the judgment merely advisory.[164]

By 1933 the Court had become more tolerant toward the "mere declaratory judgment" and actually reviewed such a proceeding on an appeal from the Supreme Court of Tennessee. Relying partially upon the ruling in the *Swope* case and using the doctrine of "substance, not form" as a lubricant to diminish the friction between conflicting decisions, the Court, in *Nashville, Chattanooga, and St. Louis R. Co. v. Wallace*,[165] sustained its jurisdiction to review declaratory judgments in cases where an injunction would issue. Here a railroad company, acting under the Tennessee uniform declaratory

[163] *Ibid.*, 131.   [164] *Ibid.*, 134.   [165] 288 U.S. 249.

judgment statute, had sought a declaration that a tax on gasoline brought by the company into the state for moving interstate trains was void as an undue interference with interstate commerce. To the contention of counsel for the state that the proceeding was a mere declaratory judgment and not a case or controversy that was cognizable in the federal courts, the Court presented a realistic front and answered with its doctrine of substance, not form, looking "not to the label which the legislature has attached to the procedure followed in the state courts, or to the description of the judgment which is brought here for review, in popular parlance, as 'declaratory,' but to the nature of the proceeding which the statute authorizes, and the effect of the judgment rendered upon the rights which the appellant asserts." [166]

Accordingly, there was no doubt that the issues raised by the suit would have constituted a case or controversy if raised and decided in a suit brought by the taxpayer to enjoin collection of the tax. There were adverse parties. Valuable legal rights were asserted and would be "directly affected to a specific and substantial degree by the decision of the question of law." The question was one of the kind traditionally decided by the Court, and the relief sought was "a definitive adjudication of the disputed constitutional right of the appellant, in the circumstances alleged, to be free from tax." Finally, there was no attempt to obtain "a decision advising what the law would be on an uncertain or hypothetical state of facts, *as was thought to be the case* [167] in *Liberty Warehouse Company v. Grannis* and *Willing v. Chicago Auditorium Association*." Thus

[166] *Ibid.*, 259.   [167] Italics are my own.

the narrow question presented for determination was whether the controversy "which would be justiciable in this Court if presented in a suit for injunction, is [was] any the less so because through a modified procedure appellant has [had] been permitted to present it in the state courts, without praying for an injunction or alleging that irreparable injury will [would] result from the collection of the tax." [168]

From the unqualified rule in *Liberty Warehouse Company v. Burley Tobacco Growers' Association* that the Supreme Court would not review a declaratory judgment, the Court evolved a rule that admitted of review in cases where an injunction would issue; and by its use of the doctrine of substance, not form, it left the door open for further modifications. The "mere declaratory judgment" in the *Willing* case had become a "label" beyond which courts would look for purposes of review.

Just why the federal courts regarded the declaratory judgment as a pernicious innovation outside the pale of the judicial function is difficult to perceive when it has met with only one reversal, and that temporary, in the courts of twenty-nine states. One of the reasons, undoubtedly, is the fear that the declaratory judgment broadens the scope of judicial review and increases the possibility of attack on the validity of legislative action. Assuming, however—and this is just what the American constitutional system does assume—that judicial review is a salutary device for the protection of constitutional rights against unauthorized legislation, then the speediest and most efficacious method possible should be provided for testing the validity of doubtful legislation. Whether

[168] (1933), 288 U.S. 249, 262–263.

the declaratory judgment will actually increase attacks on the validity of legislation is a matter of doubt because eventually a case involving legislation of doubtful validity will, in some manner, be brought to the courts for adjudication. All the declaratory judgment does, therefore, is to simplify the procedure.

That the declaratory judgment statute is not likely to be of any significant value in preventing litigation and mitigating the violence of trial by combat is manifested in the decisions of the Supreme Court arising under the Act of 1934.[169] In *Aetna Life Insurance Co. v. Haworth* [170] the Court ruled that the District Court should have issued a declaration of rights of the parties under disability benefit clauses in an insurance policy, but it went on to make the usual insistence upon adversary proceedings, justiciable controversy, and specific relief. In *Ashwander v. Tennessee Valley Authority* [171] the Court approved the refusal of the lower courts to enter a general declaratory decree concerning the rights of the TVA in all of its varied aspects because "assumed potential invasion of rights" was not enough to justify intervention, and because the declaratory judgment statute of 1934 did not purport to change the essential requisites

---

[169] The pertinent provisions of the statute follow:
"(1) In cases of actual controversy . . . the courts of the United States shall have power upon petition, declaration, complaint, or other appropriate pleadings to declare rights and other legal relations of any interested party petitioning for such declaration, whether or not further relief is or could be prayed, and such declaration shall have the force and effect of a final judgment or decree and be reviewable as such.
"(2) Further relief based on a declaratory judgment or decree may be granted whenever necessary or proper." Act of June 14, 1934, c. 512, 48 Stat. at L. 955; Judicial Code, sec. 274 D.

[170] (1937), 300 U.S. 227.   [171] (1936), 297 U.S. 288.

of judicial power but applied only to "cases of actual controversy" which connoted "a controversy of a justiciable nature" and excluded "an advisory decree upon a hypothetical state of facts." [172]

Similarly, in *United States v. West Virginia* [173] the Supreme Court refused to enter a declaratory decree adjudicating the rights of the United States and the state of West Virginia in the New and Kanawha rivers and to enjoin the construction of a dam which the United States alleged was in violation of the Federal Water Power Act. The dispute turned about the navigability of the river and the authority of the Federal Power Commission to require a license for the construction of the dam, lack of which West Virginia denied. Although an actual controversy or "the ripening seeds of one" seemed to be present, the Court found nothing to constitute a "case" or "controversy" within the meaning of the Constitution on the ground that no federal property was threatened, no interference with navigation was contemplated, and no allegation was made that the state was aiding the construction of the dam.[174] Although it was held that the United States as sovereign might have a sufficient interest in maintaining its authority over navigable waters and in enforcing the Federal Water Power Act to enable it to maintain a suit in equity to restrain threatened unlawful invasion, and that a cause of action within the jurisdiction of the District Court was stated with respect to the corporate defendants who were to construct the dam, no case with regard to the state was presented.[175]

[172] *Ibid.*, 324–325.
[174] *Ibid.*, 470–471.
[173] (1935), 295 U.S. 463.
[175] *Ibid.*, 473.

At most the bill was held to state no more than a difference of opinion between the two jurisdictions concerning the navigability of the rivers, and the judicial power did not extend to the "adjudication of such differences of opinion." Although no effort was made by the government to sustain the bill under the declaratory judgment statute, the Court noted that it was applicable only "in cases of actual controversy" and did "not purport to alter the character of the controversies which are the subject of the judicial power of the constitution." [176] Thus legal questions arising out of the intricacies of the federal system and important public and private rights were left shrouded in mysterious doubts because the United States had brought suit against the wrong party before the wrong tribunal.

Electric Bond and Share Co. v. Securities Exchange Commission [177] deserves notice because it illustrates, as well as any case, the difficulty of obtaining an adjudication on the validity of a statute when the Court does not want to give it and the difficulty of enforcing a statute until an adjudication of its validity is had. The Public Utilities Holding Company Act was passed in 1935, between which time and 1937 enforcement of the act was effectively blocked by fifty-eight injunction suits brought by holding companies, in bankruptcy in seven suits, and by stockholders in six suits.[178] Finally, in March, 1938, after a lapse of almost three years, the Supreme Court upheld those provisions of the act compelling public utility holding companies to register with the Securities Exchange Commission. However, the Court refused

---

[176] *Ibid.*, 474, 475.   [177] (1938), 303 U.S. 419.
[178] Injunctions in cases involving acts of Congress, Sen. Doc. No. 43.

to go beyond the question of the validity of the registration requirements and consider the cross bill filed by the company seeking a declaration that "each and every provision of the Act" was unconstitutional. The policy of the Court in this case provides an interesting contrast to one like *Pennsylvania and Ohio v. West Virginia*,[179] where the Court considered controversies that might never have become real. Here, however, the cross bill is not considered because it "presents a variety of hypothetical controversies which may never become real. We [the Court] are invited to enter into a speculative inquiry for the purpose of condemning statutory provisions the effect of which in concrete situations, not yet developed, cannot now be definitely perceived. We [the Court] must decline that invitation." [180]

The federal declaratory judgment has, therefore, been completely futile as a means of preventing litigation in cases involving the validity of legislation and in expediting the determination of constitutional issues involving public interests and private rights of the greatest magnitude. In no case has a declaratory judgment been issued in cases involving the validity of acts of Congress; and from the foregoing it is logical to assume that none will be issued except in cases where an injunction would issue and would suffice as it has sufficed in most of the cases involving the validity of specific items of the New Deal.

That the federal declaratory judgment is not likely to be of any great aid as an instrumentality of preventive

---

[179] (1923), 262 U.S. 553.
[180] Electric Bond and Share Co. v. Securities Exchange Commission (1938), 303 U.S. 419, 443.

justice in cases involving purely private interests is evident from the restrictions thrown about the issue of declaration of rights in *Aetna Life Insurance Co. v. Haworth*.[181] There the Court made it plain that the application of the act is governed by the limitation on the exercise of the judicial power to cases and controversies.[182] As a condition precedent to the issue of a declaration there must be a controversy that is "appropriate for judicial determination . . . a justiciable controversy is thus distinguished from a difference or dispute of a hypothetical or abstract character; from one that is academic or moot. . . . The controversy must be definite and concrete, touching the legal relations of parties having adverse legal interests. . . . It must be a real and substantial controversy admitting of specific relief through a decree of a conclusive character, as distinguished from an opinion advising what the law would be upon a hypothetical state of facts." [183]

[181] (1937), 300 U.S. 227.   [182] *Ibid.*, 239–240.

[183] *Ibid.*, 240–241. That the Court has advanced but little, if any, in its attitude toward the declaratory judgment since the Swope and Wallace cases is further manifested by the following excerpt. The declaratory judgment, said the Court, "in its limitation to 'cases of actual controversy,' manifestly has regard to the constitutional provision and is operative only in respect to controversies which are such in the constitutional sense. The word 'actual' is one of emphasis rather than of definition. Thus the operation of the Declaratory Judgment Act is procedural only. In providing remedies and defining procedure in relation to cases and controversies in the constitutional sense the Congress is acting within its delegated power over the jurisdiction of the federal courts which the Congress is authorized to establish. . . . In dealing with methods within its sphere of remedial action the Congress may create and improve as well as abolish or restrict. The Declaratory Judgment Act must be deemed to fall within this ambit of congressional power, so far as it authorizes relief which is consonant with the exercise of the judicial function in the determination of con-

All the old elements of a case emphasized since *Musk-rat v. United States* were found to be present. There was a dispute between parties in an adversary proceeding in which the parties had taken adverse positions. The insured claimed total and permanent disability, relief from the obligation to continue payments of premiums, and the consequent right to receive disability benefits. The insurance company denied all these claims and contended that the policies had lapsed. Here was a dispute that was "manifestly susceptible of judicial determination," calling "not for an advisory opinion upon a hypothetical basis but for an adjudication of present right upon established facts"; here was a case that reflected all the vestigial remains of trial by combat in which contestants fought to obtain rights. Just as people in other days believed that right would emerge victorious out of combat, we today believe that justice and truth emerge from a competition of error between lawyers who have taken the place of the champions of old. Thurman W. Arnold with wit and wisdom has summarized the attitude of the courts toward the necessity of an actual case or controversy as follows:

The ideal of the common law, dramatized over and over again by courts, expresses individual freedom from regulation. The part it plays is supposed to be the antithesis of bureaucracy—the villain of the piece. It encourages business men to fight each other for business. It encourages litigants to fight each other to obtain law. It withholds legal rights from those who will not fight. Legal rights might become cheapened if they were handed down to those who do not spend time and money to obtain them. It is beneath the dig-

---

troversies to which under the Constitution the judicial power extends." Aetna Life Insurance Co. v. Haworth (1937), 300 U.S. 227, 239-240.

nity of a court to become part of regulatory machinery, even in a supervisory capacity, unless its interest was aroused at the sight of controversy.[184]

What is the result of the Court's rigid insistence in satiating its lust for violence by having contesting parties line against each other in adverse positions over real issues? Has it accomplished its purpose of diminishing litigation in frivolous cases over abstract questions? Has it materially accomplished its purpose of limiting the rise of cases testing the validity of legislation? If not, what has it accomplished?

That the position of the Court has at times relieved it of the necessity of deciding frivolous questions like the validity of a daylight-saving time statute and embarrassing questions like the constitutionality of Justice Black's appointment is evident, but it is no more difficult to present frivolous questions in the form of a "case" than it is serious controversies. Conceding, however, that the insistence upon the necessity of a "case" has discouraged frivolous litigation, it has certainly not limited the possibilities of judicial review of legislation, and this seems to be its primary purpose. At some time, perhaps sooner, perhaps later, the question of the constitutionality of any legislation that adversely affects powerful economic interests will be presented to the Court in a "case." All that the insistence upon a proper presentation of constitutional questions has produced to date is delay, confusion, and uncertainty.

Sufficient evidence for this is found in the history of the litigation that has developed out of the activities of

[184] Thurman W. Arnold, "Trial by Combat and the New Deal" (1934), 47 Harv. L. Rev. 913, 931–932.

the New Deal. Two years elapsed between the enactment of the National Industrial Recovery Act and the
declaration by the Court that it was invalid. Three years
elapsed before the Court approved of any part of the
TVA. More than four years have elapsed since the enactment of the Public Utilities Holding Company Act,
but beyond the validity of the requirement of registration neither the Securities Exchange Commission, charged
with the enforcement of the act, nor the public utility
holding companies know their rights and duties under
the statute. It is not too adventurous to predict that at
the rate such litigation has been proceeding, it will be a
generation before even the constitutionality of much
present-day legislation is determined.

In the meantime, enforcement of regulatory legislation is obstructed by uncertainty, by attempts of the
government to avoid disadvantageous suits, and by the
use of the ever-present injunction which has been transformed from an ancillary writ incidental to the exercise
of jurisdiction previously acquired into a means of acquiring jurisdiction and a procedural device for testing
the validity of legislation and administrative regulation.
If the function of law is to provide a modicum of cer-
tainty consonant with the ends of justice, the Court's lust
for violent struggles between litigants has done much to
impair the exercise of that function.

As Professor Arnold has pointed out, "the notion that
they could decide only contested issues put the courts in
an admirable strategic position. It gave them a constant
escape from being rushed into interpretation of regulations at unpropitious times. It enabled them to take pot
shots at specific regulations without ever being forced

to assume responsibility for the regulatory scheme as a whole." [185] Through the legal device of a "case" or "controversy" the courts participate in the legislative process without participating in responsibility for legislation.

That courts in the exercise of judicial review of legislation and administrative regulation are performing legislative functions is a proposition few will deny. Indeed, most of those worthies who appeared before the Senate Judiciary Committee in 1937 to protest against the President's proposal for judicial reform did not deny this. These "Olympians" admitted that the federal courts had gone beyond the sphere of judicial propriety and rectitude. They merely objected to the method. The sham that courts have no substantive power to declare acts of a legislature unconstitutional or to exercise a suspensory veto through the device of the injunction but have only the power to apply the law to cases and controversies properly presented for adjudication has accomplished more than any other device in giving to the federal courts powers of the greatest magnitude without the slightest responsibility. The federal courts should either abandon this ceremonious pretense or be forced to do so by constitutional amendment.

The absurdity of a system which makes judicial review the keystone of the arch and permits courts by ceremonies and celebrations always to obscure and occasionally to defeat its real purposes is too manifest even for courts and judges who are apt to be "naïf, simple-minded men" and to "need something of Mephistopheles." Such celebrations recall the suggestion of Professor

[185] *Ibid.*, 934. See also *The Symbols of Government* (New Haven, 1935), chap. VIII, by the same author.

Robson that the modern lawyer is a lineal descendant of the primitive medicine man in a tribe of savages.[186] Like the medicine man of a primitive tribe, the modern judge mixes strange elements to obtain unpredictable results; he peers into present and future mysteries and solemnly chants his ritual. The primitive medicine man, however, did not always demand a combat before he would function. The instinct for violence among modern judges is more highly developed.

[186] William A. Robson, *Civilization and the Growth of Law* (New York, 1935), chap. III.

CHAPTER II

POWER OF CONGRESS TO REGULATE JURISDICTION

WIDESPREAD abuses by federal judges in the exercise of judicial power during the past fifty years have elicited a multitude of congressional proposals for curbing the powers of the federal judiciary. These proposals range all the way from proposed amendments to the Constitution which would deprive the federal courts of all power to declare acts of Congress unconstitutional to bills to withdraw jurisdiction from the courts in given classes of cases and to restrict the exercise of specific judicial powers. Many of the less drastic of these proposals have been enacted into law as in the Clayton Act, the Norris-La Guardia Act, the Johnson Act, and the Judiciary Act of 1937. Whether enacted or not, proposals to withdraw jurisdiction and restrict the exercise of judicial power always inspire strenuous and furious discourses on the question of the constitutional power of Congress to regulate the jurisdiction and powers of the federal judiciary. In recent years this question has become of vast practical importance involving not only the relationships existing between the legislative and judicial departments, but also grave issues of public policy and the maintenance of political and social democracy.

If Congress desires to limit the equity jurisdiction of

the federal courts in labor disputes, can it do so without withdrawing all diversity jurisdiction and repealing that section of the Clayton Act which gives private parties the right to seek an injunction to restrain the violation of the anti-trust laws? If, as a matter of public policy, Congress desires to withdraw equity jurisdiction in proceedings to restrain the enforcement of state statutes and the orders of state administrative bodies on the ground of repugnance to the Constitution of the United States, can it do so without depriving the federal judiciary of all jurisdiction in cases involving a federal question? What is the nature and extent of the power of Congress to define and restrict the jurisdiction and powers of courts of its own creation? When once created, do these courts receive jurisdiction and powers from the Constitution which are beyond the reach of legislative action?

Such is the nature of the questions concerning the limits of congressional authority on the one hand and the untouchable nature of the judicial power on the other. Their answers are not to be found solely by reference to the Constitution. Its provisions are vague, if not wholly silent on the subject; and the questions cannot be answered solely by a resort to general principles of constitutional theory because the theory of a paramount authority of Congress over statutory courts is incompatible with the idea of an independent judiciary and the doctrine of the separation of powers. They can only be answered by a pragmatic reference to what Congress and the courts have done with regard to these questions from the early days of the Republic to the present day.

The Constitution expressly empowers Congress "to

constitute tribunals inferior to the Supreme Court"[1] and "to make all laws which shall be necessary and proper for carrying into execution the foregoing powers, and all other powers vested by this Constitution in the Government of the United States, or in any department or officer thereof."[2] Article III, section 1, declares that "The judicial power of the United States shall be vested in one Supreme Court, and in such inferior courts as the Congress may from time to time ordain and establish." The second section of the same article provides that:

The judicial power of the United States shall extend to all cases, in law and equity, arising under this Constitution, the laws of the United States, and treaties made, or which shall be made, under their authority;—to all cases affecting ambassadors, other public ministers, and consuls;—to all cases of admiralty and maritime jurisdiction;—to controversies to which the United States shall be a party;—to controversies between two or more states,—between a State and citizens of another State,—between citizens of different States,—between citizens of the same State claiming lands under grants of different States, and between a State, or the citizens thereof, and foreign States, citizens, or subjects.

In all cases affecting ambassadors, other public ministers and consuls, and those in which a State shall be a party, the Supreme Court shall have original jurisdiction. In all the other cases before mentioned, the Supreme Court shall have appellate jurisdiction, both as to law and to fact, with such exceptions, and under such regulations as the Congress shall make.

Under the above provisions, then, Congress has express power to ordain and establish tribunals inferior to the Supreme Court, to pass all laws necessary and proper for carrying out the power vested in the judicial depart-

[1] Article I, sec. 8, cl. 9.   [2] *Ibid.*, cl. 18.

ment, and to regulate the appellate jurisdiction of the Supreme Court. However, legislative power is restrained by express prohibitions and implied limitations. In enacting legislation purporting to regulate the jurisdiction of the lower federal courts, Congress cannot pass an *ex post facto* law;[3] or abolish trials by jury in criminal cases[4] or in suits at the common law where the amount in controversy exceeds twenty dollars;[5] or abolish indictment by a grand jury in capital and other infamous crimes;[6] or deprive any person of life, liberty, or property without due process of law.[7]

Moreover, congressional power in this respect is restrained by certain implied limitations. The doctrine of the separation of powers, though not expressly contained in the Constitution, is well grounded in American constitutional law.[8] Accordingly, in establishing courts and defining and limiting their powers and jurisdiction, Congress cannot impair the corollary principle of an independent judiciary.[9] Second, it cannot impose nonjudicial functions or duties upon courts established under Article III[10] or extend their jurisdiction beyond the cases

[3] *Ibid.*, sec. 9, cl. 3.   [4] Article III, sec. 2, cl. 3, Amendment VI.
[5] *Ibid.*, Amendment VII.   [6] *Ibid.*, Amendment V.   [7] *Ibid.*
[8] The leading case is Myers v. U.S. (1926), 272 U.S. 52. See also Springer v. Government of Philippine Islands (1928), 277 U.S. 189; Evans v. Gore (1920), 253 U.S. 245; Kilbourn v. Thompson (1868), 103 U.S. 168, 190–191; Wayman v. Southard (1825), 10 Wh. 1, 42–43. However, compare Ex parte Grossman (1925), 267 U.S. 87, where the doctrine of the separation of powers was minimized to the vanishing point; see also Felix Frankfurter and James M. Landis, "Power of Congress over Procedure in Criminal Contempts in 'Inferior' Federal Courts—A Study in Separation of Powers" (1924), 37 Harv. L. Rev. 1010.
[9] Evans v. Gore (1920), 253 U.S. 245.
[10] Hayburn's Case (1792), 2 Dall. 409; U.S. v. Yale Todd (1794), not reported, see note inserted by Taney, Ch.J., in 13 How. 52; U.S.

and controversies specifically enumerated in Article III, section 2.[11] Third, Congress cannot withdraw from judicial cognizance a matter of private right, which is the subject of a suit at the common law, or in equity, or admiralty and maritime jurisdiction, and vest its final determination in an administrative or executive department.[12] Fourth, Congress cannot impair the independence of judgment of courts by imposing arbitrary rules of decision.[13] Finally, courts, as an incident of their creation and existence, possess certain implied and inherent powers essential to their existence, to the performance of judicial duty, and to the preservation of their just authority, which Congress may regulate but cannot destroy.[14]

---

v. Ferreira (1851), 13 How. 40; Gordon v. U.S. (1864), 2 Wall. 561; 117 U.S. 697; Muskrat v. U.S. (1911), 219 U.S. 346. The subject is exhaustively treated in the last case cited. See also Hunt v. Palao (1846), 4 How. 589; McNulty v. Batty (1850), 10 How. 72; U.S. v. Jones (1886), 119 U.S. 477; Baltimore & Ohio R.R. Co. v. I.C.C. (1910), 215 U.S. 216.

[11] Hodgson v. Bowerbank (1809), 5 Cr. 303, 304; Dred Scott v. Sandford (1856), 19 How. 393.

[12] Murray v. Hoboken Land & Improvement Co. (1856), 18 How. 272, 284; Crowell v. Benson (1932), 285 U.S. 22, 50–57.

[13] U.S. v. Klein (1872), 13 Wall. 128. See, however, Pennsylvania v. Wheeling and Belmont Bridge Co. (1855), 18 How. 421, where the Court upheld an act of Congress which declared lawful an obstruction which the Court had previously declared unlawful. See the same case decided in 1851, 13 How. 518.

[14] Michaelson v. U.S. (1924), 266 U.S. 42; Craig v. Hecht (1923), 263 U.S. 255; Marshall v. Gordon (1917), 243 U.S. 521; Ex parte Peterson (1920), 253 U.S. 300. Frankfurter and Landis, op. cit., 37 Harv. L. Rev. 1010, at pp. 1022–1023, deprecate the use of the term "inherent powers" and insist, quite correctly, that "The manifestation of a court's activity is not a mystical emanation inhering in the unique nature of a court; it is referable solely to the fact that a court has business in hand and must get on with it. . . . The accumulated weight of

Leaving the bare constitutional provisions which relate to legislative power over the judicial department and such abstract principles as the separation of powers and turning to acts of Congress and judicial decisions, it is apparent that the Supreme Court of the United States, by virtue of judicial precedent and historical evolution, occupies a unique position in the organization of the federal judiciary as well as in the American constitutional scheme in its entirety. The Constitution provides for "one Supreme Court," which has been held to be a constitutional as distinguished from a statutory court, although its organization and the terms of its sitting depend upon congressional enactment.[15] Acting upon the theory that its own existence is established by the Constitution, the Supreme Court has held that its grant of original jurisdiction is self-executing and that after its organization by the Act of 1789 it could proceed to exercise such jurisdiction without further congressional enactment prescribing jurisdiction and regulating procedure.[16] This construction of the Court's power was

---

repetition behind such a phrase as 'inherent powers' of the lower Federal Courts is a constant invitation to think words instead of things."

[15] The organization of the Supreme Court is provided for in sec. 215, Judicial Code; sec. 321 U.S.C. Section 230 of the Judicial Code (sec. 338 U.S.C.) requires the Court to hold one term annually at the seat of government beginning on the first Monday in October and such adjourned or special terms as it may find necessary. In 1802, to prevent the Supreme Court from passing on the act abolishing the courts and judgeships created by the Act of 1801, Congress set February, 1803, as the date for the next term, and thereby omitted the August term, 1802. See Carpenter, *Judicial Tenure in the United States*, 76.

[16] Chisholm v. Georgia (1793), 2 Dall. 419; Rhode Island v. Massachusetts (1838), 12 Pet. 657; Florida v. Georgia (1854), 17 How. 478; Kentucky v. Dennison (1860), 24 How. 66, 96.

definitely adopted in 1793 in the great case of *Chisholm v. Georgia*,[17] which was an action of assumpsit brought originally in the Supreme Court by a citizen of another state against the state of Georgia. Although section 13 of the Judiciary Act of 1789 provided that the Court should have exclusive jurisdiction of all cases of a civil nature in which a state was a party except between a state and its citizens and between a state and citizens of another state or aliens, in which latter case it should have original and not exclusive jurisdiction, Congress had not authorized an action of assumpsit against a state and had not prescribed forms of process for the Court in the exercise of its original jurisdiction. Nevertheless, Chief Justice Jay and Justices Wilson and Cushing upheld the jurisdiction of the Court. Justice Iredell dissented on the ground that Congress had not authorized and could not authorize an action of assumpsit against a state and that the grant of original jurisdiction in Article III was not self-executing. "I conceive, that all the courts of the United States must receive, not merely their *organization* as to the number of judges of which they are to consist; but all their authority, as to the manner of their proceeding, from the legislature only. This appears to me to be one of those cases, with many others, in which an article of the constitution cannot be effectuated without the intervention of the legislative authority." [18] Almost seventy years

[17] 2 Dall. 419.

[18] *Ibid.*, 432. Prior to the Chisholm case the Supreme Court exercised its original jurisdiction in two other cases without any legislation other than the Act of 1789. The first was in 1792 in Georgia v. Brailsford, 2 Dall. 402, and the other in Oswold v. State of Georgia, cited by Ch.J. Taney in Kentucky v. Dennison, 24 How. 66. In neither of these cases did the question of jurisdiction arise. By taking jurisdiction, however, the Court decided the question.

later in *Kentucky v. Dennison*,[19] Chief Justice Taney reviewed the authorities and regarded the matter as settled that in all cases where original jurisdiction is given by the Constitution, the Supreme Court has authority "to exercise it without any further Act of Congress to regulate its process or confer jurisdiction; and that the Court may regulate and mold the process it uses in such manner as in its judgment will best promote the purposes of justice."

Since the Supreme Court derives its original jurisdiction by direct grant from the Constitution, it follows that Congress can neither enlarge [20] nor restrict that jurisdiction.[21] Although it is subject to no limitations other than those expressed in the Constitution, it is not exclusive, and Congress may vest such jurisdiction concurrently in the lower federal courts so long as it does not impair the constitutional grant of power in Article III. Thus, a consul may be sued in the lower federal courts if the requisite diversity of citizenship exists,[22] and a suit brought by a state in its own courts may be removed to an inferior federal tribunal under the removal acts.[23] Of

---

[19] (1860), 24 How. 66, 98.
[20] Marbury v. Madison (1803), 1 Cr. 137.
[21] Wisconsin v. Pelican Insurance Co. (1888), 127 U.S. 265.
[22] Bors v. Preston (1884), 111 U.S. 252.
[23] Ames v. Kansas ex rel. Johnston (1889), 11 U.S. 449. See also U.S. v. Ortega (1826), 11 Wh. 467; Gittings v. Cramford (1838), Fed. Case No. 5,465. On the power of Congress to invest the lower federal courts with concurrent jurisdiction of those cases in which the Supreme Court has original jurisdiction, see further United States v. California (1936), 297 U.S. 175. See also Ohio ex rel. Popovici v. Agler (1930), 280 U.S. 379, to the effect that the vesting of original jurisdiction of cases involving ambassadors and other public ministers did not deprive the state courts of jurisdiction of such cases. This case involved a divorce decree entered by a state court against a Rumanian consul in

the exercise of this power by Congress, Chief Justice Waite said:

It rests with the Legislature to say to what extent such grants shall be made, and it may safely be assumed that nothing will ever be done to encroach upon the high privilege of those for whose protection the constitutional provision was intended. At any rate, we are unwilling to say that the power to make the grant does not exist.[24]

Unlike its original jurisdiction, the appellate jurisdiction of the Supreme Court of the United States is subject to an almost complete control by Congress because of the provision that such jurisdiction is exercised subject to such exceptions and under such regulations as Congress shall make; and the grant of appellate jurisdiction is not self-executing. Although it would appear from the words of Article III that the power of Congress in this respect is wholly negative in character, the effect of judicial decisions is the contrary. Statutes affirmatively conferring appellate jurisdiction upon the Supreme Court have been held to exclude its exercise in all cases in which it is not affirmatively and expressly granted.[25] In other words, an affirmative bestowal of appellate jurisdiction is exclusive in character and automatically constitutes an exception to all other cases.

This has been the rule since 1796, when in *Wiscart v. D'Auchy* [26] the Court held that since Congress had prescribed no rule for appellate proceedings in the Court, it

---

Cleveland. The Supreme Court refused to hear his case protesting against the decree for lack of jurisdiction of the state court.

[24] Ames v. Kansas (1884), 111 U.S. 449, 469.

[25] Wiscart v. D'Auchy (1796), 3 Dall. 321; Durousseau v. U.S. (1810), 6 Cr. 307; Ex parte McCardle (1869), 7 Wall. 506.

[26] *Supra.*

could exercise no appellate jurisdiction, and that if a rule were prescribed the Court could not depart from it. Justice Wilson took exception to this view and argued that since the Court's appellate jurisdiction was derived from the Constitution, it could be exercised without an act of Congress in view of Congress' failure to make exceptions to its exercise. Similarly, in *Durousseau v. United States* [27] Chief Justice Marshall, speaking for the Court, averred that the appellate powers of the Court were derived from the Constitution and not from an act of Congress. Nevertheless, he went on to hold that since Congress had affirmatively defined the appellate jurisdiction of the Court, without making exceptions to it, the affirmative description of appellate powers implied a negative of all others.[28]

Congress can even deprive the Supreme Court of jurisdiction in cases pending before it. The most extreme exercise of congressional authority in this respect occurred in 1869 in the great case of *Ex parte McCardle*.[29] Here a newspaper editor filed a petition in the United States Circuit Court for the Southern District of Mississippi alleging unlawful restraint by the military force acting under the Reconstruction Acts. The writ was issued, and a return was made by the military commander who admitted the restraint but denied that it was unlawful in view of the incendiary and libelous newspaper articles alleged to have been written by the petitioner. Upon hearing, the prisoner was remanded to the custody of the military authorities, but he was allowed an appeal to the Supreme Court of the United States and admitted to bail.

[27] *Supra.*   [28] *Supra.*   [29] 7 Wall. 506.

The Supreme Court denied a motion to dismiss the appeal, heard argument on the merits of the case, and took it under advisement.[30] While the case was thus pending and before a conference could be held regarding a decision, Congress became fearful of a test of the validity of the Reconstruction Acts and enacted a law in 1868 which deprived the Court of its appellate jurisdiction of the case.[31] Chief Justice Chase, speaking for the Court, reaffirmed the doctrine that the affirmative bestowal of appellate jurisdiction implied a negation of all other such jurisdiction and dismissed the appeal. He said:

Without jurisdiction the Court cannot proceed at all in any cause. Jurisdiction is the power to declare the law and when it ceases to exist, the only function remaining to the Court is that of announcing the fact and dismissing the cause.[32]

Although the rule of the *McCardle* case had its origin in the storm and stress of the Civil War and the Court wilted—as it must always wilt—in the heat generated by a serious and determined congressional majority, continued repetition and approval of the principles enunciated therein have made the *McCardle* case good law. Accordingly, no doubt exists, in so far as the judicial article is concerned, of the unlimited discretionary power

[30] Ex parte McCardle (1867), 6 Wall. 318.
[31] Act of March 27, 1868, 15 Stat. at L. 44.
[32] On this point the Court, referring to earlier cases, said: "This principle that the affirmation of appellate jurisdiction implies the negation of all such jurisdiction not affirmed having been thus established, it was an almost necessary consequence that Acts of Congress, providing for the exercise of jurisdiction, should come to be spoken of as Acts granting jurisdiction, and not as Acts making exceptions to the constitutional grant of it."

of Congress to curtail and abolish the appellate jurisdiction of the Supreme Court and to prescribe the manner and forms in which the Supreme Court may exercise
such jurisdiction.[33]

One other case of legislative and judicial conflict in
which the Supreme Court yielded to Congress deserves
consideration. In 1852 the Supreme Court took original
jurisdiction of a suit in equity brought by the state of
Pennsylvania for the removal of a certain bridge over
the Ohio River which was alleged to be an unlawful
obstruction to navigation. After taking voluminous testimony the Court found that the bridge was an unlawful
obstruction and directed its removal either by elevation
to a designated height or by abatement.[34] Shortly after
the rendition of this decree Congress enacted a law de-
claring the bridge in question and others to be lawful
structures, designating them as post roads, and requiring
vessels navigating the river not to interfere with the
elevation or construction of bridges.[35] In 1856, again in
the exercise of its original jurisdiction,[36] the Supreme

[33] Colorado Central Mining Co. v. Turck (1893), 150 U.S. 138, 141;
National Exchange Bank v. Peters (1891), 144 U.S. 570, 572; The
Francis Wright (1881), 105 U.S. 381, 385–386; American Construction
Co. v. Jacksonville, T. & K. W. R. Co. (1892), 148 U.S. 378. See especially Ex parte Yerger (1868), 8 Wall. 77, 104–106. For earlier cases
see Barry v. Merclin (1847), 5 How. 103, 119; Crawford v. Points
(1851), 13 How. 11.

[34] Pennsylvania v. Wheeling and Belmont Bridge Co. (1852), 13
How. 518.

[35] Act of August 31, 1852, c. 3, sec. 6, 10 Stat. 110, 112.

[36] Pennsylvania v. Wheeling and Belmont Bridge Co. (1856), 18
How. 421. This case is also important as a construction of the original
equity jurisdiction of the Supreme Court of which Nelson, J., speaking
for the Court, said:
"Original jurisdiction in equity in a particular class of cases conferred by the Constitution on this court, has been interpreted to im-

Court upheld the act of Congress on the ground that there was "no longer any interference with the enjoyment of the public right inconsistent with law." The Court clung to the general proposition that an act of Congress could not operate to annul the judgment of the Supreme Court, but it distinguished between the decree previously rendered and a judgment in an action at law in a case of private right where a judgment for damages would have passed beyond the control of Congress.

As regards the organization and jurisdiction of the lower federal courts, legislative enactments and judicial decisions point to a plenary power in Congress to create and abolish such courts at its discretion. As an incident to this power, statutes and precedents affirm the paramount authority of Congress to regulate the jurisdiction, procedure, and powers of the inferior federal tribunals. Nevertheless, the indiscriminate use of such mystical phrases as inherent powers along with metaphorical utterances to the effect that Congress may not interrupt the flow of the stream of judicial power into the vessel of jurisdiction have so beclouded the issues that doubts have arisen concerning the authority of Congress to limit the jurisdiction and powers of courts of its own creation. Moreover, the complete evisceration of various statutes purporting to restrict the powers of the lower federal

---

pose the duty to adjudicate according to such rules and principles as governed the action of the Court of Chancery in England, which administered equity at the time of the emigration of our ancestors, and down to the period when our Constitution of the United States conferred that jurisdiction on this court, it cannot be construed to exclude power possessed and constantly exercised by every court of equity then known, to use its discretion to award or refuse costs, as its judgment of the right of the case in that particular might require." P. 462.

courts suggests that such statutes would be unconstitutional unless construed strictly.

Since 1789 two theories of congressional authority over the jurisdiction of the lower federal courts have persisted. The first theory, which may be called the congressional theory since it attributes to Congress a broad authority over the federal courts, runs to the effect that by virtue of its power to constitute tribunals inferior to the Supreme Court, the Congress has complete power to withhold from the lower courts jurisdiction of those cases enumerated in Article III, section 2, and that no such court may exercise any jurisdiction not expressly conferred by statutory enactment. The second theory, which may be called the Story theory since it was best formulated in the ascetic legalism of Justice Story, runs to the effect that Congress not only is obliged to create courts inferior to the Supreme Court, but that it has no power to withhold jurisdiction from the courts in those cases to which the judicial power of the United States is extended by Article III. Stated in another way, the Story theory, as it has evolved to the present, means that the lower federal courts receive their jurisdiction and powers from the Constitution and not from statutory enactment and, consequently, that Congress has no power to define or describe the jurisdiction and power of courts of its own creation once they have been established. It is due to the rugged persistence of this theory for 144 years that it is necessary to examine acts of Congress and decisions of the Supreme Court over the same period in order to determine where congressional authority ends and judicial power begins.

From the very birth of the federal government until the present day Congress has entertained a broad view of its powers over the organization, jurisdiction, powers, and procedure of the lower federal courts; and, as a practical matter, the Supreme Court has acquiesced in this view because there is not one single case where it has declared unconstitutional an act of Congress which purported to limit the jurisdiction and powers of the lower federal courts. The debate in the Senate and the House over the Judiciary Act of 1789, the provisions of the act itself, and, even more important, its omissions are all recognitions of the correctness of the congressional theory as opposed to the court or Story theory.

During the debate on the judiciary bill two general groups appeared. The federalists or pro-constitutionalists took the view that Congress could not withhold from the courts the jurisdiction specified in Article III.[37] The other group consisted of extreme advocates of states' rights and opponents of the new constitution who wished either to confine the jurisdiction of the federal courts within narrow limits or to refuse to provide for courts inferior to the Supreme Court altogether and vest their original jurisdiction in the state courts with only appellate jurisdiction vested in the Supreme Court of the United States.[38] Neither group prevailed in its views, but the compromise reached was an express recognition by legislative construction of the theory of broad congressional power upon which the opponents of a strong federal judiciary based their contentions.

[37] For an excellent account of the debate in the Senate on the Judiciary Act of 1789, see Charles Warren, "New Light on the History of the Judiciary Act of 1789" (1923), 37 Harv. L. Rev. 49.

[38] Ibid., 62, 63, 65–66, 67–68.

In the second place, the proposed equity jurisdiction of the federal courts in section 16 of the draft bill met heavy opposition. Some senators such as Paterson, Johnson, Lee, Grayson, and Maclay opposed all equity jurisdiction; [39] and so anxious was the Senate, as a whole, to preserve the right of trial by jury that at one time it amended the draft bill so as to require a jury trial of facts in cases in equity. This amendment, however, was later expunged by the Senate on July 10, 1789.[40] The debate in the House added nothing to what was said in the Senate regarding the power of the legislature over the lower federal courts and revealed the same general views.[41] The debates in Congress over the judiciary bill are significant in that they contain the well-considered opinions of many who were members of the Philadelphia Convention and of the ratifying conventions, and also because they reveal that Congress, at least, entertained no delusions concerning inherent equity powers or the self-executing nature of the grant of judicial power.

Even more significant is the act itself. It specified the times and places of holding court, not only for the circuit and district courts, but for the Supreme Court as well; provided for adjournment of the Supreme Court; [42] empowered the Supreme Court and district courts to appoint clerks; [43] conferred original jurisdiction upon the district and circuit courts in certain cases; [44] vested the

[39] *Ibid.*, 96–100.

[40] *Ibid.*, 79, 99. See also Senate Journal, July 10, 1789.

[41] For a consideration of the constitutional aspects of legislative power over jurisdiction in the House, see the account of the speech of Representative Johnson on August 1, 1789. 1 Annals of Congress, 854–855.

[42] Secs. 1, 3, 5, 6, Act of Sept. 24, 1789, 1 Stat. at L. 73.

[43] Sec. 7, *ibid.*   [44] Secs. 9–12, *ibid.*

Supreme Court with original jurisdiction and empowered it to issue writs of mandamus; [45] empowered the courts of the United States to issue certain writs in aid of their jurisdiction,[46] to compel the attendance of witnesses and giving of testimony,[47] to grant new trials, punish contempts of their authority, and make all necessary rules for the orderly conduct of their business; [48] and so on. These grants of power and jurisdiction, commonly viewed as inherent in courts, demonstrate conclusively that the First Congress deemed positive action on its part necessary before such power and jurisdiction could be exercised by the federal courts.

The Act of 1789 is also important for its omissions in certain instances and for the restrictions it imposed in others. Congress failed altogether to confer original jurisdiction upon the federal courts in cases arising under the Constitution, laws, and treaties of the United States. Except for the brief period between the enactment of the Act of 1801 and its repeal in 1802, the lower federal courts had no jurisdiction in that very important group of cases involving a federal question, and it was not until 1875 that they were vested with judicial power over such cases.[49] In the second place, diverse citizenship jurisdiction in suits at the common law or in equity was limited to cases in which an amount exceeding five hundred dollars was involved, subject to the proviso that no circuit or district court should take cognizance of a suit to recover the contents of any promissory note or other chose in action in favor of an assignee, unless such

[45] Sec. 13, *ibid.*   [46] Sec. 14, *ibid.*
[47] Sec. 15, *ibid.*   [48] Sec. 17, *ibid.*
[49] Act of March 3, 1875, c. 137, 18 Stat. at L. 470. See Warren, "New Light on the History of the Judiciary Act of 1789," *loc. cit.*, 62.

a suit might have been instituted prior to the assignment,[50] excepting foreign bills of exchange. Except for the raising of the jurisdictional amount, these provisions have remained in force ever since their enactment, so that at no time in the history of the federal judiciary have the lower courts been vested with all the jurisdiction that the Constitution gives them the capacity to receive. The equity jurisdiction of the circuit and district courts was limited to those cases in which a plain, adequate, and complete remedy could not be had at law,[51] and the mode of proof by oral testimony and examination of witnesses in open court was made the same in all federal courts in actions of equity as well as in suits at law.[52] Finally, the power to issue writs was limited to cases in aid of the jurisdiction of the courts and, in habeas corpus proceedings, to prisoners confined under or by color of the authority of the United States.[53]

Ever since this practical legislative construction of Article III by the First Congress, the national legislature has always proceeded upon the assumption that it had complete discretion to regulate and restrain the jurisdiction, powers, and procedure of the lower federal courts. But Congress has not been alone in this broad construction of its powers relating to the organization, jurisdiction, and procedure of the lower federal judiciary. As early as 1799 in the case of *Turner v. Bank of North*

[50] Sec. 11. For an interesting account of the origin of the amount in controversy limitation, see Warren, "New Light on the History of the Judiciary Act of 1789," *loc. cit.*, 78. It appears that the limitation was designed to keep heirs of Lord Fairfax from suing in the federal courts on quit rents. See also the speech of Representative Nicholas, of Virginia, in the House on January 7, 1801, 6th Cong., 2nd Sess., on a bill to reduce the jurisdictional amount to four hundred dollars.

[51] Sec. 16.   [52] Sec. 30.   [53] Sec. 14.

America,[54] the Supreme Court of the United States concurred in this view. The case involved an attempt to recover on a promissory note and the application of section 11 of the Judiciary Act of 1789, which forbade such suits in diverse citizenship jurisdiction in favor of an assignee unless the suit could have been brought before the assignment had been made. Counsel for the bank contended that the Circuit Court was not technically an inferior court and that the judicial power of the United States was a direct grant of jurisdiction to the courts by the Constitution and one which Congress could neither limit nor enlarge. Chief Justice Ellsworth interrupted him at this juncture and asked if the federal courts might "exercise a jurisdiction, without the intervention of the legislature, to distribute and regulate the power," and Justice Chase interposed to say:

> The notion has frequently been entertained, that the federal courts derive their power immediately from the Constitution; but the political truth is, that the disposal of the judicial power (except in a few specified instances) belongs to Congress. If Congress has given the power to this Court, we possess it, not otherwise, or to any other court, it still remains at the legislative disposal. Besides Congress is not bound, and it would, perhaps, be inexpedient, to enlarge the jurisdiction of the federal courts to every subject, in every form, which the Constitution might warrant.[55]

Counsel pursued the same line of argument, but the Court applied section 11 of the Judiciary Act and thereby gave judicial expression to the proposition that the federal courts have no jurisdiction not conferred by an act of Congress. Eight years later in *Ex parte Bollman* [56]

[54] 4 Dall. 8.   [55] *Ibid.*, 10.   [56] (1807), 4 Cr. 75.

Chief Justice Marshall laid down the definite rule that "Courts which originate in the common law possess a jurisdiction which must be regulated by the common law, until some statute shall change their established principles; but courts which are created by written law, and whose jurisdiction is defined by written law, cannot transcend that jurisdiction." [57] In 1812, in the famous case of *United States v. Hudson and Goodwin*,[58] the Supreme Court reaffirmed this rule on the ground that the power which Congress possesses to create courts inferior to the Supreme Court necessarily implied "the power to limit the jurisdiction of those courts to particular objects," [59] and held that the federal courts had no common-law jurisdiction in criminal cases.

[57] *Ibid.*, 93. See also Bank of U.S. v. Deveaux (1809), 5 Cr. 61, where it was held that the right to sue does not imply a right to sue in the federal courts unless expressed in an act of Congress.

[58] 7 Cr. 32.

[59] *Ibid.*, 33. "When a court is created, and its operations confined to certain specific objects, with what propriety," asked the Court, "can it assume to itself a jurisdiction—much more extended; in its very nature very indefinite; applicable to a great variety of subjects; varying in every state in the Union—and with regard to which there exists no definite criterion of distribution between the district and circuit courts of the same district?"

The reasoning of Justice Johnson is interesting. The judicial power of the United States "is to be exercised by courts organized for the purpose, and brought into existence by an effort of the legislative power of the Union." Only the Supreme Court possesses jurisdiction derived immediately from the Constitution, of which the legislature cannot deprive it. "All other courts created by the general government possess no jurisdiction but what is given them by the power that creates them, and can be vested with none but what the power ceded to the general government will authorize them to confer." P. 33. Though federal courts have certain implied powers to punish for contempt and enforce the observance of order in their presence, such powers do not extend to the punishment of violations against the peace and dignity of the sovereign power. P. 34. Compare the language of

The most sweeping assertion of legislative power by the Supreme Court was made in 1845 in *Cary v. Curtis*.[60] In reply to the argument of counsel that an act of Congress which made the decision of the Secretary of the Treasury final in tax disputes was unconstitutional because it deprived the courts of the judicial power vested in them by the Constitution and conferred it upon an executive officer, the Court, speaking through Justice Daniel, replied that:

. . . the judicial power of the United States, although it has its origin in the Constitution, is (except in enumerated instances applicable exclusively to this court), dependent for its distribution and organization, and for the modes of its exercise, entirely upon the action of Congress, who possess the sole power of creating tribunals (inferior to the Supreme Court), for the exercise of the judicial power, and of investing them with jurisdiction either limited, concurrent, or exclusive, and of withholding jurisdiction from them in the exact degrees and character which to Congress may seem proper for the public good.[61]

Baldwin, J., in Rhode Island v. Massachusetts (1838), 12 Pet. 657, 721–722, to the effect that "the distribution and appropriate exercise of the judicial power must therefore be made by laws passed by Congress, and cannot be assumed by any other department, else, the power being concurrent in the legislative and judicial departments, a conflict between them would be probable, if not unavoidable, under a constitution or government which made it the duty of the judicial power to decide all cases in law or equity arising under it, or laws passed, and treaties made by its authority."

[60] 3 How. 236.

[61] *Ibid.*, 245. Continuing, the Court said: "To deny this position would be to elevate the judicial over the legislative branch of the government, and to give to the former powers limited by its own discretion merely. It follows, then, that the courts created by statute, must look to the statute as the warrant for their authority; certainly they cannot go beyond the statute, and assert an authority with which they may not be invested by it, or which may be clearly denied to them. This argument is in nowise impaired by admitting that the judicial

Five years later the same principle was applied in *Sheldon v. Sill* [62] in which the validity of section 11 of the Judiciary Act of 1789 was directly put in question. The assignee of a negotiable instrument filed a suit in equity in the United States Circuit Court for the District of New York even though no diversity of citizenship existed as between the original parties to the mortgage. The Court took jurisdiction of the case and decreed a sale of the property in question contrary to the prohibition of section 11 of the original judiciary act. On appeal to the Supreme Court, counsel for assignee asserted that section 11 was void because the right of a citizen of one state to sue citizens of another state in the federal courts in all cases was given directly by the Constitution, and consequently that Congress could not restrict that right [63] or deprive the courts of the judicial power vested in them by the Constitution.[64] In reply to these arguments the Court held that since the Constitution had not established the inferior courts or distributed

---

power shall extend to all cases arising under the Constitution and laws of the United States. Perfectly consistent with such an admission is the truth, that the organization of the judicial power, the definition and distribution of the subjects of jurisdiction in the federal tribunals, and the modes of their action and authority, have been, and of right must be the work of the legislature. The existence of the judicial act itself, with its several supplements, furnishes proof unanswerable on this point. The courts of the United States are all limited in their nature and constitution, and have not the powers in courts existing by prescription or by the common law." P. 245. In vigorous dissents, Justices Story and McLean denied the authority of Congress to take away the power of the courts and vest it in an executive officer on the ground that "the right to construe the laws in all matters of controversy is of the very essence of judicial power." Such an assumption of power by Congress, they contended, violated the principle of the separation of powers, impaired the independence of the judiciary, and joined the executive and judicial departments.

[62] (1850), 8 How. 441.   [63] *Ibid.*, 442.   [64] *Ibid.*, 446–447.

to them their respective powers, Congress, having the
authority to establish the courts, could define their jurisdiction and withhold from any court of its creation jurisdiction of any of the enumerated cases and controversies
in Article III. Although the Constitution had defined the
judicial power of the United States, it had not prescribed
how much of it should be exercised by the circuit courts.
Consequently, a statute prescribing the limits to jurisdiction could not conflict with the Constitution unless
it conferred jurisdiction not enumerated in Article III.
Accordingly, courts created by statute have no jurisdiction other than the statute confers, and no court can assert a claim to jurisdiction "exclusively conferred on
another, or withheld from all." [65]

To consider further cases to this effect is but to em-
phasize the cumulative effect of precedent. *Sheldon v.
Sill* has been cited, quoted, and reaffirmed in numerous
cases.[66] The total effect of all of them is that as regards
the jurisdiction of the inferior federal courts two ele-

[65] *Ibid.*, 449.

[66] Ladew v. Tennessee Copper Co. (1910), 216 U.S. 357, 358; Mayor
v. Cooper (1867), 6 Wall. 247, 251–252; Ex parte Yerger (1868), 8
Wall. 77, 104; Gaines v. Fuentes (1875), 92 U.S. 10, 18; Rice v. M. & N.
R.R. Co. (1861), 1 Bl. 358, 374; Stevenson v. Fain (1904), 195 U.S. 165,
167; Kentucky v. Powers (1906), 201 U.S. 1, 24; U.S. v. Eckford (1867),
6 Wall. 484, 488; Jones v. U.S. (1890), 137 U.S. 202, 211; Case of the
Sewing Machine Companies (1873), 18 Wall. 553, 557–558; Holmes v.
Goldsmith (1893), 147 U.S. 150, 158; Venner v. Great Northern R.
Co. (1908), 209 U.S. 24, 35; Johnson Company v. Wharton (1894),
152 U.S. 252, 260; Kline v. Burke Construction Co. (1922), 260 U.S.
226, 233, 234; Plaquemines Tropical Fruit Co. v. Henderson (1898),
170 U.S. 511, 513–521; Morgan v. Gay (1874), 19 Wall. 81, 83. For
other cases prior to Sheldon v. Sill, see Bank of U.S. v. Deveaux (1809),
5 Cr. 61; (1817), 2 Wh. 369; McIntire v. Wood (1813), 7 Cr. 504, 506;
McCluny v. Silliman (1817), 2 Wh. 369; U.S. v. Nourse (1832), 6 Pet.
470, 495; Kendall v. U.S. (1838), 12 Pet. 524, 616; U.S. v. Bevans
(1818), 3 Wh. 336.

ments are necessary to confer jurisdiction. First, the Constitution must have given the courts the capacity to receive it, and, second, an act of Congress must have conferred it. As stated by Justice Swayne,[67] "Their concurrence is necessary to vest it. It is the duty of Congress to act for that purpose up to the limits of the granted power. They may fall short of it, but cannot exceed it. To the extent that such action is not taken, the power lies dormant. It can be brought into activity in no other way." The manner in which the lower federal courts acquire jurisdiction, its character, the mode of its exercise, and the objects of its operation are submitted "without check or limitation to the wisdom of the legislature." [68] This power is incidental to the absolute power of Congress to create and abolish at will tribunals inferior to the Supreme Court, and limitations to its exercise must be found elsewhere than in Article III.[69] Jurisdiction having been conferred may be taken away in whole or in part as Congress in the exercise of its discretion may deem expedient, and all pending cases,

[67] Mayor v. Cooper (1867), 6 Wall. 247, 252.

[68] *Ibid.*, 251–252. Cf. the language of Sutherland, J., in Kline v. Burke Construction Co. (1922), 260 U.S. 226, 234. As recently as 1934, Justice McReynolds, as spokesman of the Court, said: "The accepted doctrine is that the lower federal courts were created by the acts of Congress and their powers and duties depend upon the acts which called them into existence, or subsequent ones which extend or limit. . . . Whatever may be the inherent power of a court incident to a grant of jurisdiction . . . there seems no ground whatever for saying that Congress cannot withhold or withdraw from courts of equity the right to empower receivers in conservation proceedings to disregard local statutes." Gillis v. State of California, 293 U.S. 62, 66.

[69] Kline v. Burke Construction Co., *supra*, 234. See also Assessor v. Osborne (1869), 9 Wall. 567, 575; Norris v. Crocker (1851), 13 How. 429, 440; Merchant's Ins. Co. v. Ritchie (1867), 5 Wall. 541; Hallowell v. Commons (1916), 239 U.S. 506.

though cognizable when commenced, are withdrawn from further consideration by the courts. Litigants have no inherent right to sue in the federal courts regardless of the character of the parties or the nature of the controversy. Such right can only be found in the statutes, and what the statute may give, it may take away.[70] Since the Constitution extends the judicial power to nine classes of cases at law and in equity, Congress may withhold, in whole or in part, jurisdiction in any or all of these classes. It may confer jurisdiction in all such cases at law and withhold it in the same cases in equity. It may create a separate system of law and chancery courts and vest in them law and equity jurisdiction respectively, or it may abolish completely the whole inferior federal judiciary and leave the judicial power of the United

[70] Kline v. Burke Construction Co., *supra*, 233. See also Myers v. U.S. (1926), 272 U.S. 52, 130, where, in answer to an argument of counsel, the Court responded that the power of Congress to regulate removals was not analogous to its power to establish tribunals inferior to the Supreme Court. The Court regarded the classes of cases enumerated in Article III as "a description and reservoir of the judicial power of the United States and a boundary of that federal power as between the United States and the states, and the field of jurisdiction within the limits of which Congress may vest particular jurisdiction in any one inferior federal court which it may constitute."

Continuing, the Chief Justice remarked:

"It is clear that the mere establishment of a federal inferior court does not vest that court with all the judicial power of the United States as conferred in the second section of Article 3, but only that conferred by Congress specifically on the particular court. It must be limited territorially and in the classes of cases to be heard, and the mere creation of the courts does not confer jurisdiction, except as it is conferred in the law of its creation or its amendments." P. 130. Judicial power, therefore, is vested only in the courts and is to be distributed to particular courts and conferred or withheld at the discretion of Congress. Even if Congress were duty bound to vest the whole judicial power in the courts of its creation, such a duty would be one of imperfect obligation and therefore unenforceable. *Ibid*.

States unexecuted. Such would seem to be the necessary effect of the cases just cited and reviewed. Constitutional law, however, is to a large extent a synthesis of antagonistic elements. In no class of cases is this union of theses and antitheses more apparent than in the cases dealing with the judicial power.

The foregoing view, therefore, presents but one aspect of the complex and many-sided picture of the judicial power. In the first place, none of the principles stated in *Sheldon v. Sill* and succeeding cases applies to the regulation of the admiralty and maritime jurisdiction. For some reason, as yet unrevealed by judicial decision, the determination of the nature and extent of the admiralty jurisdiction is the function of the courts and not of Congress. As stated by the Court in the case of *The Lottawanna*,[71] "The question as to the true limits of maritime law and admiralty jurisdiction is undoubtedly . . . exclusively a judicial question, and no state law or act of Congress can make it broader, or (it may be added) narrower than the judicial power may determine these limits to be."

In the second place, there have arisen certain theories of the judicial power to the effect that, once created

---

[71] (1875), 21 Wall. 558. Compare the language of Chief Justice Taney in "The St. Lawrence," 1 Bl. 526, 527, when, in speaking of the admiralty jurisdiction, he said, "but certainly no state law can enlarge it, nor can an act of Congress or rule of court make it broader than the judicial power may determine to be its true limits."

Congress, however, may change the substantive law of admiralty and regulate the forms of procedure in admiralty cases. Crowell v. Benson (1932), 285 U.S. 22, 53–56; The Genesee Chief, 12 How. 443; In re Garnett (1891), 141 U.S. 1, 12. For the general nature and extent of the admiralty and maritime jurisdiction, see The Belfast (1869), 7 Wall. 624, 627; Detroit Trust Co. v. The Thomas Barlum (1934), 293 U.S. 21, 43–44.

and invested with jurisdiction, courts cannot be abolished and their jurisdiction cannot be diminished unless substitutes are provided. These contentions have their source in judicial opinions, in the expressions of the Senate lawyers, and in arguments of counsel. Their general acceptance would, of necessity, result in the establishment and perpetuation of a judicial oligarchy at which Congress could not strike. The continued reiteration and stubborn persistence of such legalistic theories of inherent jurisdiction provide a useful instrument in the hands of judges for the assertion of judicial prerogative against legislative fiat.

The principal source of the theory of oligarchical court power is *Martin v. Hunter's Lessee*.[72] In this case Justice Story went out of his way to write an essay on the judicial power in which he undertook to lecture Congress on its moral duties under Article III. Starting with the proposition that the mandatory force of Article III was "so imperative, that Congress could not, without violation of its duty, have refused to carry it into operation," Story proceeded, with what Justice Johnson characterized as "hypercritical severity in examining the distinct force of words," [73] to place great emphasis upon the words "shall be vested" and "shall extend." "The judicial power must, therefore, be vested in some court, by Congress; and to suppose that it was not an obligation binding them, but might, at their pleasure, be omitted or declined, is to suppose that under the sanction of the

[72] (1816), 1 Wh. 304, 329–336.
[73] *Ibid.*, 374. Dissenting opinion. Justice Johnson denied that the words "shall extend" necessarily meant "shall include in." "The plain and obvious meaning of the word *shall*, in this sentence," he said, "is in the future sense, and has nothing imperative about it." P. 374.

Constitution, they might defeat the Constitution itself; a construction which would lead to such a result cannot be sound."

The judicial power, he went on to argue, is as absolutely vested in courts as the legislative power is in Congress, and Congress is obliged to create inferior courts in which to vest all of the jurisdiction that they are capable of receiving. "If, then," he said, "it is a duty of Congress to vest the judicial power of the United States, it is a duty to vest the whole judicial power. The language, if imperative as to one part, is imperative as to all. If it were otherwise, this anomaly would exist, that Congress might successively refuse to vest the jurisdiction in any one class of cases enumerated in the Constitution, and thereby defeat jurisdiction as to all; for the Constitution has not singled out any class on which Congress are bound to act in preference to others."

In the whole of his homily on the duty of Congress to create courts and vest in them all of the judicial power they are capable of exercising, Story never went further than to say that such was a moral as distinguished from a legal obligation. At no time did he intimate that the judicial power was self-executing or that once courts were created they were automatically endowed with the jurisdiction of all cases to which the judicial power extends. Indeed, he expressly recognized that Congress might establish one or more inferior courts and "parcel out the jurisdiction among such courts, from time to time, at their own pleasure." All, therefore, that Story was contending for was the federalistic principle that "the whole judicial power of the United States should be, at all times, vested, either in an original or appellate form, in some courts created under its authority." [74] In other words, as he stated further in his opinion:

> The original or appellate jurisdiction ought not, therefore, to be restrained, but should be commensurate with the mischiefs intended to be remedied, and of course, should extend to all cases whatsoever.[75]

Story, therefore, was merely stating with added emphasis the principle first enumerated in the eightieth number of *The Federalist* and later incorporated in judicial decisions that "the judicial power of every well-constituted government must be co-extensive with the legislative, and must be capable of deciding every question which grows out of the Constitution and laws." [76] He was, then, stating a political axiom rather than enunciating a rule of law. In spite of the fact that Story meant no more than a moral obligation by his references to the duty of Congress to vest all the judicial power in some courts, *Martin v. Hunter's Lessee* is the foundation of all arguments against the complete power of Congress to regulate the jurisdiction of the lower federal courts.

A second line of cases that is used by the partisans of a federal judiciary beyond the range of legislative control is that beginning with *Murray v. Hoboken Land and Improvement Co.*[77] and ending with *Crowell v. Benson.*[78] The former case involved the constitutional authority of Congress to empower the Secretary of the

---

[74] *Ibid.,* 331.   [75] *Ibid.,* 335.

[76] Cohens v. Virginia (1811), 6 Wh. 264, 384; Kendall v. U.S., 12 Pet. 527. "All governments," said Chief Justice Marshall in Osborn v. Bank of United States (1824), 9 Wh. 738, 818, 819, "which are not extremely defective in their organization, must possess within themselves, the means of expounding, as well as enforcing their own laws."

[77] (1856), 18 How. 272.   [78] (1933), 285 U.S. 22.

Treasury to sell·the lands of a defaulting collector of revenue for the purpose of recovering collections due the United States. In answer to the argument of counsel that the issuance of the distress warrant by the solicitor of the treasury was a judicial function that could only be performed by courts exercising the judicial power, the Court upheld the act of Congress but accepted the underlying assumption of the argument by observing that Congress could not withdraw from judicial cognizance a matter which, from its nature, was the subject of a suit at the common law, or in equity, or admiralty. On the other hand, matters of public right susceptible of, but not requiring, judicial determination might or might not be brought within judicial cognizance as Congress in its discretion might provide. This dictum of Justice Curtis constituted a serious limitation upon the sweeping assertion of congressional power over the jurisdiction of the lower federal courts in *Cary v. Curtis* and suggested that in some matters, at least, Congress was bound to provide judicial remedies. The total effect of the dictum was not made clear until three-quarters of a century later when the Court, in *Crowell v. Benson,* considered the power of Congress to vest final determination of jurisdictional facts arising in workmen's compensation cases under the longshoremen's and harbor workers' act in an executive official.

Crowell, a deputy compensation commissioner, had found that an employee of Benson had been injured in the course of his employment on the navigable waters of the United States and that the relation of master and servant existed. Basing its reasoning partly upon the due process clause of the Fifth Amendment, but more especially upon the dictum in the *Murray* case, the Court, in an elaborate opinion written by Chief Justice Hughes, construed the statute so as to permit a trial *de novo* of mixed questions of law and fact arising under the Constitution and sustained the action of the District Court in retrying the jurisdictional facts. The Court drew a sharp distinction between determinations of fact in cases of private right and those in cases arising between the government and persons subject to its authority in connection with the performance of its constitutional functions and ruled that the suit in question was a case in admiralty involving a private right. Thus far, then, the case would seem to relate solely to the power of Congress to amend the maritime laws and regulate the procedure of the courts in admiralty cases within the limits of the due process clause of the Fifth Amendment, but the Chief Justice chose to base his opinion on a broader ground.

Conceding the power of Congress to revise the maritime law and prescribe the forms of procedure in admiralty cases, the Court went on to indicate that in so doing Congress could not "reach beyond the limits which are inherent in the admiralty and maritime jurisdiction." In other words, the power of Congress and of the commissioner was dependent upon the fact of where the injury occurred and further upon the existence of the relationship of master and servant. In relation to these facts the Court insisted that the question did not concern the propriety of administrative finality or simply that of due process of law as regards notice and hearing. It was "rather a question of the appropriate maintenance of the Federal judicial power in requiring the observance of Constitutional restrictions," and "whether the Congress may substitute for constitutional courts, in which the judicial power of the United States is vested, an administrative agency—in this instance a single deputy commissioner—for the final determination of the existence of the facts upon which the enforcement of the constitutional rights of the citizen depend."

Congress, therefore, cannot completely deprive the courts of all power to determine facts by vesting their determination in its own instrumentalities because that "would be to sap the judicial power as it exists under the Federal Constitution and to establish a government of a bureaucratic character alien to our system, wherever fundamental rights depend, as not infrequently they do depend, upon the facts, and finality as to facts becomes in effect finality in law." [79]

What, then, is the combined effect of the *Murray* and *Crowell* cases? As regards the judicial power alone it is simply that Congress cannot withdraw from judicial cognizance matters of private right to which the judicial power of the United States extends and vest them in legislative agencies or executive bodies. The implications of the *Crowell* case are more far reaching, however. The emphasis upon the function of the federal judicial power in requiring the observance of constitutional limitations for the enforcement of the constitutional rights of the citizen contains the suggestion that the citizen has a right to bring suit in the federal courts to protect them, and that, consequently, Congress must, to satisfy the minimum demands of due process, provide protection for such rights by creating courts with jurisdiction in such

[79] *Ibid.*, 56–57.

cases as may involve the fundamental rights of the individual.[80]

This conclusion is buttressed by the statement that:

In cases brought to enforce constitutional rights, the judicial power of the United States necessarily extends to the independent determination of all questions, both of fact and law, necessary to the performance of that supreme function. The case of confiscation is illustrative, the ultimate conclusion almost invariably depending upon questions of fact. This court has held the owner to be entitled to a fair opportunity for submitting that issue to a judicial tribunal for determination upon its own independent judgment as to both law and facts.[81]

Thus, "the essential independence of the judicial power of the United States in the enforcement of constitutional rights" requires an independent trial of constitu-

[80] Cf. Truax v. Corrigan (1921), 257 U.S. 312, where an Arizona law limiting the use of the labor injunction was declared invalid upon the ground, among others, that the due process clause of the Fourteenth Amendment requires a "minimum of protection for every one's right of life, liberty and property, which the Congress or the legislature may not withhold."

[81] Crowell v. Benson, *supra*, 64; citing Ohio Valley Water Co. v. Ben Avon Borough (1920), 253 U.S. 287. To these views Justice Brandeis, with whom concurred Justices Stone and Roberts, dissented. "The 'judicial power' of Article III," contended the dissenters, "is the power of the federal government, and not of any inferior tribunal. There is nothing in that article which requires any controversy to be determined as of first instance in the federal district courts. The jurisdiction of those courts is subject to the control of Congress." P. 86. Citing Turner v. Bank of North America, 4 Dall. 8, 10; U.S. v. Hudson, 7 Cr. 32, 33; Sheldon v. Sill, 8 How. 441, 449; Justices v. Murray, 19 Wall. 274, 280; Home Life Insurance Co. v. Dunn, 19 Wall. 214, 226; Stevenson v. Fain, 195 U.S. 165, 167; Kline v. Burke Construction Co., 260 U.S. 226, 234; Frankfurter and Landis, *The Business of the Supreme Court*, 65–68; Charles Warren, "Federal Criminal Laws and the State Courts," 38 Harv. L. Rev. 545.

tional issues by a court of the United States upon its own record.

That the Supreme Court of the United States intends to persist in its determination to require a trial *de novo* of jurisdictional facts of a constitutional nature is substantiated by the strong language of Chief Justice Hughes in *St. Joseph Stockyards Co. v. United States*.[82] The underlying assumption of the Chief Justice in this case, as in the *Crowell* case, is that courts—and only courts—as the repositories of all that is wise and good, are the only agencies that can or will protect the constitutional rights of persons. Legislatures and legislative agencies, contends the Chief Justice, "with varying qualifications, work in a field peculiarly exposed to political demands. Some may be expert and impartial, others subservient." To make their findings of fact conclusive where constitutional rights are involved would be "to place those rights at the mercy of administrative officials and seriously to impair the security inherent in judicial safeguards. That prospect with our multiplication of administrative agencies is one not to be lightly regarded. Under our system there is no warrant for the view that the judicial power of a competent tribunal can be circumscribed by a legislative arrangement designed to give effect to administrative action going beyond the limits of constitutional authority." [83] Thus the rule of law is utilized to buttress and fortify the rule of judges.

[82] (1936), 298 U.S. 38.
[83] *Supra*, 51–52. Justice Brandeis, in a separate concurring opinion, exposed briefly but adequately the sophistry of the Chief Justice when he said: "The supremacy of law demands there shall be opportunity to have some court decide whether an erroneous rule of law was ap-

Other cases lend support to the view that the citizen is entitled to seek the protection of his constitutional rights and the enforcement of constitutional guaranties in the regularly constituted federal courts exercising independently the judicial power of the United States. In *Irvine v. Marshall* [84] the Court made it explicit that the jurisdiction of the federal courts is commensurate "with every right and duty created, declared or necessarily implied by and under the Constitution and laws of the United States." Even more significant is *Truax v. Corrigan* [85] involving the validity of an act of the Arizona legislature which limited the use of the injunction in labor disputes and legalized picketing so long as violence was not used. The act was annulled as a violation of the equal protection of the laws and as a denial of due process of law. The due process clause was held to require that "every man shall have the protection of his day in court, and the benefit of the general law, a law which hears before it condemns, which proceeds not arbitrarily or capriciously, and renders judgment only after trial, so that every citizen shall hold his life, liberty, property and immunities under the protection of the general rules which govern society. It of course tends to secure equality of law in the sense that it makes a required minimum of protection for every one's right of life, liberty, and property, which the Congress or the legislature may not withhold." [86]

---

plied and whether the proceeding in which facts were adjudicated was conducted regularly. . . . But supremacy of law does not demand that the correctness of every finding of fact to which the rule of law is to be applied shall be subjected to review by a court." *Supra,* 84.

[84] (1857), 20 How. 558.   [85] (1921), 257 U.S. 312.

[86] *Ibid.,* 332, citing Hurtado v. California, 110 U.S. 516, 535. Compare

In this case the required minimum of protection was the issuance of an injunction by a court of equity to restrain picketers from peaceably persuading patrons to boycott a restaurant. In general, such a minimum, under this rule, would be the right of the individual to resort to the courts for the protection of his life, liberty, and property not only as against encroachment by the government but also as against violation by other individuals. Any act, therefore, which withholds or fails to extend such protection is held as falling short of the requirements of due process. If, therefore, government

---

In re Opinion of the Justices (1931), 176 N.E. 649, where the Supreme Court of Massachusetts held unconstitutional as a violation of due process of law the provisions of a proposed bill which limited the equity powers of the courts in labor disputes and withdrew legal and equitable protection from the yellow-dog contract. Cases cited as authorities for this conclusion were Adair v. U.S., 208 U.S. 161; Coppage v. Kansas, 236 U.S. 1; Truax v. Raich, 239 U.S. 33; New York Central R. Co. v. White, 243 U.S. 188; Hitchman Coal and Coke Co. v. Mitchell, 245 U.S. 229; Prudential Ins. Co. v. Cheek, 259 U.S. 530; Adkins v. Children's Hospital, 261 U.S. 525; Highland v. Russel Car Co., 279 U.S. 253. See also the advisory opinion of the same court In re Opinion of the Justices (1930), 171 N.E. 234, where similar proposals were held to be void under the Fourteenth Amendment of the Federal Constitution. Of Truax v. Corrigan, Professor Thomas Reed Powell has aptly said: "The Truax case makes one wonder at what the Supreme Court would do if Congress should forbid the federal courts to issue injunctions in cases in which the Supreme Court thinks injunctions ought to issue. There would not be the equal protection clause to invoke, but it has been hinted that severe inequalities would offend due process of law, and Congress is restrained by a due process clause. There is the principle of the separation of powers to invoke if the court thinks that the legislature has sought to deprive it of something which is the essence of judicial power. The jurisdiction of the lower federal courts may be restricted by Congress, but the Supreme Court has declared that Congress is restricted in prescribing how jurisdiction once conferred shall be exercised."

"The Supreme Court's Control over the Issue of Injunctions in Labor Disputes," 13 Proceedings, Academy of Political Science, 37, 73.

is to be administered at all, the courts must be admitted into the participation of what they deem their appropriate function in the process of government.

The element common to all of the above cases is the assertion of a constitutional right infringed or about to be infringed by some legislative act. A further common element is found in the direct rulings of some of these cases and in the intimations of others that due process guarantees the rights of the individual to resort to the courts for the protection of such rights. In the *Crowell* case the enforcement of constitutional limitations for the preservation of fundamental rights is regarded as the supreme function of courts, the performance of which is required in the independent exercise of the judicial power. The *Crowell* case, therefore, affords the basis for the assertion of the existence of an inherent jurisdiction in the federal courts, although it does not in terms state such a thesis.

In no case, however, has the Court advanced in express terms the theory of an inherent jurisdiction, and, indeed, all decisions are to the contrary. In *Turner v. Bank of North America* [87] and *Sheldon v. Sill*,[88] the Court rejected the contentions of counsel that Article III conferred a right to sue in the federal courts and ruled that the lower federal courts had no jurisdiction other than that conferred by statute. Both of these cases, however, involved the validity of the eleventh section of the original judiciary act, which prohibited the assignee of a promissory note or other negotiable instrument from bringing suits in the federal courts because of diversity of citizenship unless the original parties to the transac-

[87] (1799), 4 Dall. 8.   [88] (1850), 8 How. 441.

tion were citizens of different states. No questions of constitutional right were involved or alleged as was the case in *Crowell v. Benson* and *Truax v. Corrigan*, the plain effect of which is to infer that in some cases the Constitution confers a right upon the citizen to resort to the courts.

It is true that in *United States v. Detroit Timber and Lumber Co.*[89] the Court approached a theory of inherent equity jurisdiction in the courts. Here a bill in equity had been filed to cancel certain patents to timber lands because of fraud, some of which had been sold to a bona fide purchaser. The District Court cancelled the patents, but the Circuit Court of Appeals modified the decree so as to permit the purchaser in good faith to hold the lands. The modified decree was affirmed by a unanimous court, which, speaking through Justice Brewer, said:

It is a mistake to suppose that, for the determination of equities and equitable rights we must look only to the statutes of Congress. The principles of equity exist independently of and anterior to, all congressional legislation, and the statutes are either enunciations of those principles or limitations upon their application in particular cases.

That the courts could apply such pre-existing principles of equity without jurisdiction over the parties or the subject matter, or that Congress could not limit or modify such principles is nowhere suggested and indeed the inference is to the contrary.

One of the few authentic and outright assertions by a judge of the Supreme Court of an inherent jurisdiction in the federal courts is contained in the dissenting opinion of Justice Pitney, with whom concurred Justices

[89] (1906), 200 U.S. 321, 339.

McKenna and Van Devanter, in *Paine Lumber Co. v. Neal*,[90] where the lumber company had sought an injunction under section 20 of the Clayton Act to restrain Neal and a carpenter's union from acting in concert to prevent the use of nonunion-made materials in other states. The majority of the Court regarded section 20 of the Clayton Act, conferring upon private parties the right to institute suits in equity to restrain violations of the act, as an expansion of the equity jurisdiction of the courts in suits arising out of the anti-trust laws [91] but held that the acts complained of did not come within the purview of the statute.

Because Justice Pitney's assertions are the best expression of the views of those who argue that the federal courts possess inherent equity jurisdiction and powers beyond the reach of legislative enactment, they may be considered at length. Beginning with the less extreme statement that, "in absence of some provisions to the contrary, the right to relief by injunction, where irreparable injury is threatened through violation of property rights, and there is no adequate remedy at law, rests upon settled principles of equity that were recognized in the constitutional grant of jurisdiction to the courts of the United States," [92] he proceeded to the broader gen-

[90] (1917), 244 U.S. 459.

[91] For a contrary view see Duplex Printing Co. v. Deering (1921), 254 U.S. 443, 471–472, where section 20 was regarded as "an exceptional and extraordinary restriction upon the equity powers of the courts of the United States . . . in the nature of a special privilege or immunity to a special class." See Professor Powell's comments in the essay cited above, 13 Proc., Acad. Pol. Sci., 37, 53. Cf. Frankfurter and Green, "Labor Injunctions and Federal Legislation" (1929), 42 Harv. L. Rev. 766.

[92] 244 U.S. 459, 473.

eralization that Article III had the effect of adopting equitable remedies in cases involving a federal question. Speaking of Article III, section 2, he said:

This had the effect of adopting equitable remedies in all cases arising under the Constitution and laws of the United States, where such remedies are appropriate. The Federal courts, in exercising their jurisdiction, are not limited to the remedies existing in the courts of the states, but are to grant relief in equity according to the principles and practice of the equity jurisdiction as established in England.[93]

Although no one would object to the latter part of this statement, it does not follow that "it is not the statute that gives a right to relief in equity, but the fact that in the particular case, the threatening effects of a continuing violation of the statute are such as only equitable process can prevent. The right to equitable relief does not depend upon the nature or source of the substantive right whose violation is threatened, but upon the consequences that will flow from its violation." [94]

Justice Pitney's argument amounts in effect to a plea for an unlimited discretion in the courts to afford equitable relief. *Truax v. Corrigan* is the answer to this plea because, as Professor Powell has correctly indicated,[95] it leads to the inference that the lower federal courts have power to issue an injunction in cases in which the Supreme Court thinks they should issue. To afford equitable relief, however, the courts must have jurisdiction over either the parties or the subject matter. They can only exercise such jurisdiction as is conferred by statute. Thus the result of the *Truax* and the *Crowell* cases would

[93] *Ibid.*, 475–476, citing Robinson v. Campbell, 3 Wh. 212, 221, 223; U.S. v. Howland, 4 Wh. 108, 115; Irvine v. Marshall, 20 How. 558, 565.
[94] 244 U.S. 459, 476.   [95] *Op. cit.*, 73 ff.

seem to be that once having conferred jurisdiction upon the courts, Congress cannot determine how it shall be exercised or withdraw it without providing sufficient remedies.

The most articulate assertions of judicial power are made not by the courts but by the lawyers practicing before them and by partisans of the courts in Congress and before congressional committees. In *Martin v. Hunter's Lessee* it was the counsel who suggested to Story the obligatory force of the words "shall extend" in Article III. In *Turner v. Bank of North America* [96] Rawle, for the defendant, argued that the judicial power in the sense of jurisdiction was a grant to the circuit courts which Congress could neither limit nor enlarge. The circuit courts, he contended, were courts of general jurisdiction similar to the King's Bench and could, therefore, exercise jurisdiction without a statutory grant. Similarly, in *Sheldon v. Sill*,[97] counsel for appellants asserted that section 11 of the Judiciary Act was void because the right of a citizen of one state to sue a citizen of another state in the federal courts in all cases was given directly by the Constitution and could not be restricted or abridged by Congress, which, although it might create courts, could not deprive them of the judicial power vested in them by the Constitution. Consequently, if Congress could not extend the original jurisdiction of the Supreme Court beyond the terms of the Constitution, it could no more take away a constitutional power than confer an unconstitutional one.

[96] (1799), 4 Dall. 8, 10.
[97] (1850), 8 How. 441, 442, 443, 446–447.

Counsel, striving to docket losing cases in the federal courts, have not been alone in their assertions of judicial prerogative. A perusal of hearings before the judiciary committees of the Senate and House of Representatives reveals that the opposition to any restriction of the jurisdiction and powers of the federal judiciary comes primarily from the representatives of large corporate business interests of an interstate or national character. They make no attempt to conceal their motives in the premises but tend to base their arguments on constitutional objections to bills designed to curb federal jurisdiction. Economic interests are thereby endowed with the sacred aura of the Constitution, and commercial aspirations become associated with patriotic efforts to preserve the independence of the judiciary.[98]

The most articulate defender of the judicial power as opposed to legislative regulation and control over the judiciary has been Mr. Alfred P. Thom, long-time legislative counsel, or lobbyist, for the railroad interests. In 1912 he appeared before the Senate Committee on the Judiciary to argue against the validity of certain proposals aimed at depriving the federal courts of the power to restrain the enforcement of state statutes and the orders of state administrative bodies.[99] In 1928 he directed the same arguments against a proposal to limit the equity

[98] Hearings before the House Judiciary Committee on H.R. 10594, 4526, and 11508, 70th Cong., 1st Sess.; "Limiting Scope of Injunction in Labor Disputes"—Hearings before Sub-committee, Senate Committee on the Judiciary, 70th Cong., 1st Sess.; Hearings on S. 937, 939, 3243, 72nd Cong., 1st Sess.

[99] "The Judicial Power and the Power of Congress in its Relation to the United States Courts," 62nd Cong., 2nd Sess., Sen. Doc. No. 443, referred to hereafter as Thom.

powers of the federal courts in labor disputes.[100] The kernel of Mr. Thom's argument is that Congress had the constitutional duty to establish courts and vest them with jurisdiction. Once having created courts and vested them with jurisdiction it takes an affirmative act to destroy them, and such, therefore, would be an unconstitutional exercise of power unless Congress created other courts. Congress, then, has no power to destroy the judicial system and consequently no power to deprive such courts that it has established of "any power essential to their completeness and competency to exercise effectively the judicial power to the extent that it has already been conferred by the Constitution." [101] Moreover, Congress cannot withdraw from the courts the power to protect the constitutional rights of the citizen against invasion. Since the method of protecting constitutional rights is nearly always the injunction, there is no other adequate remedy. The courts, it would appear from this argument, are endowed by the Constitution with adequate power to protect constitutional rights. Furthermore, the judicial power extends to cases in equity as well as to cases in law. Consequently, to destroy the efficiency of the equity power by depriving courts of the means to prevent the invasion of constitutional rights would be to destroy a substantive portion of the judicial power and impair the efficiency of the judiciary as a coordinate and essential department of the constitutional scheme.[102]

Sweeping assertions of judicial power have likewise

[100] Hearings before Sub-committee, Senate Committee on the Judiciary, 70th Cong., 1st Sess.

[101] Thom, *op. cit.*   [102] *Ibid.*, 9–13.

been made in the halls of Congress from 1789 until the present. An elaborate discussion of legislative authority to restrict the jurisdiction of the courts is contained in the debate over the Hepburn bill of 1906 in the course of the consideration of Senator Bailey's amendment to deprive the courts of power to enjoin the enforcement of orders of the Interstate Commerce Commission.[103] Senator Spooner made a distinction between jurisdiction and judicial power and proposed that "when Congress confers *jurisdiction* upon the inferior courts of the United States over any one of the cases or controversies enumerated by the Constitution, the judicial power, *ex necessitate rei*, goes with it, including the instrumentalities which inhere in the jurisdiction and are necessary to its efficient exercise." In other words, Congress may withhold jurisdiction, but it may not withhold judicial power where jurisdiction exists because such would be to impair the independence of the judiciary. Since Congress cannot determine how jurisdiction shall be exercised once it has been conferred, the argument runs, it cannot deprive courts of their power to afford preventive relief which is inherent in equity, as in admiralty, and cannot be determined by Congress but is always a judicial question.[104]

More than two decades after the historic debate over the Hepburn bill, Senator Vandenberg argued in opposition to the Norris anti-injunction bill that "Congress

[103] Speeches of March 22, 23, 1906, 40 Cong. Rec. 4115–4122, 4156; April 26, 27, 40 Cong. Rec. 5887–5899, 5945–5953. See also the remarks of Senators Culberson, 40 Cong. Rec. 3681; Knox, 40 Cong. Rec. 4382 ff.; Stone, 40 Cong. Rec. 4771–4773. See, too, Senator Bailey's reply on April 10, 1906, 40 Cong. Rec. 4977–4988.

[104] 40 Cong. Rec. 4116, 4117, 4127, 4156, 4161, 5894–5895.

is the potter which shapes the vase, but when it is shaped, the judicial power is poured into it by the Constitution and not by Congress"; [105] and Representative Beck, in one of his characteristic roles as defender of the Constitution, contended that the power to issue injunctions "in cases where a court had reason to apprehend imminent and irreparable damage was directly vested by the Constitution itself in the federal courts as an inherent power." [106] Congress, Mr. Beck observed, cannot destroy the judicial power and "where the necessary effect of any legislation is to destroy wholly the inherent and fundamental powers of the court to discharge its exalted function of administering justice, it infringes upon that 'judicial power' which, under the Constitution, is vested in the Federal courts." [107]

Even more extreme was the argument of Senator Austin in opposition to the Johnson bill to oust the federal courts of jurisdiction to enjoin the enforcement of an administrative body of a state in which jurisdiction is

[105] March 1, 1932, 75 Cong. Rec. 5004. For the entire debate in the Senate, see the Cong. Rec. for February 24, 25, and March 1, 1932.

[106] March 8, 1932, 75 Cong. Rec. 5475.

[107] *Ibid.*, 5476. Continuing, Mr. Beck said:

"For Congress to abolish the inferior Federal Courts, practically the only sources of original jurisdiction, and to refuse to substitute others, would not only be unconstitutional, but an act of revolution. . . . That the power to restrain by injunction is inherent in equity courts and is of the very essence of judicial power is clear from all the authorities and was expressly affirmed by the Debs Case. I, therefore, submit that Congress cannot, certainly as to existing courts, so impinge upon their inherent equity powers by any regulation of their procedure as to destroy altogether the power of the court to vindicate its existence and discharge its exalted functions, and that an act which forbids the issuance of a restraining order, often essential to the power of the court to do ultimate justice by final decree, would sap the very foundation of judicial authority, and to that extent, destroy the 'judicial power' thus vested by the Constitution." P. 5477.

based solely upon diversity of citizenship or the repugnancy of such order to the Federal Constitution. Assuming, as a major premise, that "the jurisdiction of the Federal courts is commensurate with every right and duty created, declared, or necessarily implied by and under the Federal Constitution and laws," [108] Senator Austin concluded that the federal courts had an inherent power to determine cases arising under the Constitution and laws of the United States [109] and to administer uniformly federal law in every state in the Union.[110] Any attempt to deprive the federal courts of this power would not only be in derogation of Article III, but would also be in violation of the guarantee of due process of law in the Fifth Amendment.[111]

Such is the nature of the transformations of the Story theory of the moral duty of Congress to create inferior federal courts and invest them with all jurisdiction which the third article of the Constitution enabled them to receive into a theory which, if accepted by the courts, would perpetuate a judicial oligarchy beyond the control of Congress and endow courts of the United States with vast inherent powers derived immediately from the Constitution. The theory is primarily the work of the lawyers in and out of Congress; it represents the lawyer's ideal of a government in which doctrinaire legalism dominates policies and in which lawyers take precedence over politicians.

Their theory, of course, differs widely from that originally expounded by Justice Story. Emphasis is shifted

---

[108] 78 Cong. Rec. 2052. See also the speech of Senator Logan for a complete perversion of the Story thesis.
[109] *Ibid.*, 2053.   [110] *Ibid.*, 2054.   [111] *Ibid.*

from all cases to cases in equity. Due process of law is used to support contentions which cases interpreting the judicial article deny. The power of a court of equity to issue the ancillary writ of injunction in aid of its jurisdiction is broadened into the power of a court of equity to issue the writ of injunction to acquire jurisdiction. Inherent equity powers are asserted. Finally, the theory of an independent prerogative of the federal courts to determine all cases involving a federal question and to administer federal law is advanced.

Such assertions are, of course, at variance with the rule discussed earlier in this chapter that the effect of Article III "is not to vest jurisdiction in the inferior courts over the designated cases and controversies, but to delimit those in respect to which Congress may confer jurisdiction upon such courts as it creates. Only the jurisdiction of the Supreme Court is derived directly from the Constitution. Every other court created by the general government derives its jurisdiction wholly from the authority of Congress. That body may give, withhold, or restrict such jurisdiction at its discretion, provided it be not extended beyond the boundaries fixed by the Constitution." [112]

The theory of an independent judicial prerogative is unsupported by other cases. In the first place, the Supreme Court has made no distinction between jurisdiction and judicial power in so finely drawn terms or in such a sense as Senators Spooner, Knox, and Culberson contended in 1906. Jurisdiction has been defined as "the power to hear and determine the subject matter in con-

[112] Kline v. Burke Construction Co. (1922), 260 U.S. 226, 234.

troversy between parties to a suit, to adjudicate or exercise any judicial power over them," [113] and as the power "to entertain a suit, consider the merits, that is, the various elements which enter into and qualify the plaintiff's rights to the relief sought, and to render a binding decision thereon." [114] Jurisdiction, then, is nothing more or less than the authority of a court to hear a case or controversy between adverse parties and pronounce a binding decision thereon.[115] Similar to the above definitions of jurisdiction are the definitions of judicial power. Justice Miller, in his well-known definition of judicial power, regarded it as "the power of a court to decide and pronounce a judgment and carry it into effect between persons and parties who bring a case before it for decision." [116] In *Muskrat v. United States* [117] Justice Day defined judicial power as "the right to determine actual controversies arising between adverse litigants duly instituted in courts of proper jurisdiction."

The Supreme Court, therefore, has defined jurisdiction and judicial power in terms of each other. It has never

[113] Rhode Island v. Massachusetts (1838), 12 Pet. 657, 718.

[114] General Investment Co. v. N.Y. Central R. Co. (1925), 271 U.S. 228.

[115] Fair v. Kohler Die and Specialty Co. (1913), 228 U.S. 22; Overby v. Gordon (1900), 177 U.S. 214; Binderup v. Pathe Exchange (1923), 263 U.S. 291; Erickson v. U.S. (1924), 264 U.S. 246; Wedding v. Meyler (1904), 192 U.S. 573; Geneva Furniture Co. v. Karpen Brothers (1915), 238 U.S. 254; Ex parte Reed (1879), 100 U.S. 13; Illinois Central R. Co. v. Adams (1901), 180 U.S. 28; Riggs v. Johnson County (1867), 6 Wall. 166; Cooper v. Reynolds (1870), 10 Wall. 308; Kendall v. U.S. (1838), 12 Pet. 524; U.S. v. Arredondo (1832), 6 Pet. 691; Grignon v. Astor (1844), 2 How. 319.

[116] *Miller on the Constitution,* quoted in Muskrat v. U.S. (1911), 219 U.S. 346, 356.

[117] 219 U.S. 346, 361.

made such a distinction between the two that would leave jurisdiction to the discretion of Congress and withdraw the judicial power from the scope of statutory regulation. Jurisdiction, of course, is a prerequisite to any exercise of the judicial power. It is the grist which feeds the mill, and without jurisdiction the judicial power must remain inert and dormant. Jurisdiction is the right of a court to exercise judicial power in a particular case. Judicial power is the general power exercised by a court when it takes jurisdiction of a case, decides it on its merits, renders a final and binding judgment, and issues process to enforce the results of its jurisdiction. It is the generic or universal power of courts of which jurisdiction is a particular manifestation.

The advocates of judicial prerogative are right, therefore, when they contend that Congress cannot compel courts to take jurisdiction of a case from which any essential elements of the judicial power have been abstracted. They err, however, when they contend that such powers attach to courts contrary to statute. Jurisdiction in cases from which essential elements of the judicial power have been withdrawn is a nonentity. The courts have no power in such cases and can exercise none. The case of *Gordon v. United States* [118] is a typical case. There, finality of judgment was withheld from the Court of Claims and the Supreme Court. The latter body did not proceed to take jurisdiction of the case and enter a final judgment therein contrary to the terms of the statute. It merely declined to take jurisdiction.

Moreover, the equitable writ of injunction, like the common-law writ of mandamus, is an ancillary writ which

[118] (1864), 117 U.S. app. 697.

can be used in aid of, but not in acquiring, jurisdiction.[119] Courts of the United States, with the solitary exception of the courts of the District of Columbia,[120] are all courts of special as distinguished from courts of general jurisdiction or of prescription.[121] Accordingly, courts created by statute must look to that statute for their authority and powers. They cannot go beyond the statute and assert powers which it clearly denies to them. They have not the powers which inhere in courts existing by prescription or by the common law.[122] The jurisdiction of the inferior courts of the United States is, therefore, determined by statute, and apart from the powers that inhere in a judicial tribunal after it has been established, they can exercise no jurisdiction not conferred upon them.[123]

Finally, the Supreme Court has never, in words, asserted a rule of inherent equity jurisdiction other than to affirm the existence of certain inherent equity powers in the federal courts for the purpose of protecting or preserving jurisdiction already acquired against interference by state courts,[124] for the prevention of the ad-

[119] McIntire v. Wood (1813), 7 Cr. 504; McClung v. Silliman (1821), 6 Wh. 598; Kendall v. U.S. (1838), 12 Pet. 524.

[120] Kendall v. U.S., *supra*.

[121] Dred Scott v. Sandford (1856), 19 How. 393, 401; Turner v. Bank of North America (1799), 4 Dall. 8, 11; Ex parte Bollman (1830), 4 Cr. 75, 93; McCormick v. Sullivant (1825), 10 Wh. 192; Kempe v. Kennedy (1809), 5 Cr. 173, 185; Rice v. M. & N. R.R. Co. (1861), 1 Bl. 358, 374.

[122] Cary v. Curtis (1845), 3 How. 236, 245; Ex parte Bollman, *supra;* Case of the Sewing Machine Companies (1874), 18 Wall. 553.

[123] Ladew v. Tennessee Copper Co. (1910), 218 U.S. 357, 358.

[124] Kline v. Burke Construction Co. (1922), 260 U.S. 226, 229; Julian v. Central Trust Co. (1904), 193 U.S. 93; Covell v. Heyman (1884), 111 U.S. 176, 182.

ministration and enforcement of its rules and practice such as would cause hardship and injustice,[125] and for the correction of what has been wrongfully done under its process.[126] As put by the Court in *Gumbel v. Pitkin*,[127] "The equitable powers of courts of law over their own process to prevent abuses, oppression and injustice are inherent and are as extensive and efficient as is their power to protect their own jurisdiction and officers in possession of property in legal custody."

What courts say, however, is often at variance with what they actually do, and their deeds frequently belie their words. In the exaggerated metaphor of Judge Baker in the *Michaelson* case,[128] it may be true, then, that as regards equity jurisdiction, Congress "can, as a potter, shape the vessel of jurisdiction, the capacity to receive; but, the vessel having been made, the judicial power of the United States is poured into the vessel, large or small, not by Congress, but by the Constitution." The strict construction of statutes purporting to restrict the powers of the courts in injunction suits, the ignoring of statutory provisions in some cases, and the attempts of the Court to avoid serious constitutional issues in cases involving statutes restricting the scope of equity jurisdiction tend indirectly to confirm a theory of inherent equity jurisdiction, although the Court has never held invalid any of the numerous restrictions imposed by Congress upon the exercise of equity powers.

The first important restriction on the equity jurisdic-

[125] Eberly v. Moore (1861), 24 How. 147.
[126] Arkadelphia Milling Co. v. St. Louis S.W.R. Co. (1919), 249 U.S. 134; Gagnon v. U.S. (1904), 193 U.S. 45.
[127] (1888), 124 U.S. 131.
[128] Michaelson v. U.S. (C.C.A., 7th Cir., 1923), 291 Fed. 940, 946.

tion of the federal courts was contained in section 16 of
the Judiciary Act of 1789, which provided that no suit
in equity should be maintained where there was a full
and adequate remedy at law. As early as 1830 the Supreme Court, in *Boyce's Executors v. Grundy*,[129] construed this provision as being merely declaratory of a
pre-existing rule long applied in chancery and, therefore,
as making no alteration in rules of equity on the subject
of legal remedies. Having mitigated the potential effects
of the restriction in this manner, the Court proceeded to
weaken it further by laying down the rule that "it is not
enough that there is a remedy at law; it must be plain
and adequate, or, in other words, as practical, and efficient to the ends of justice and its prompt administration,
as the remedy in equity." [130]

To prevent interference by federal courts with proceedings in the courts of the several states, Congress in
1793 enacted a law which provided that the writ of injunction should not be "granted by any court of the
United States to stay proceedings in any court of a State,
except in cases where such injunctions may be authorized
by any law relating to proceedings in bankruptcy." [131]
The Supreme Court has applied the spirit of the Act of
1793 with a fair degree of consistency,[132] but it has held

[129] 3 Pet. 210.   [130] *Ibid.*, 215.
[131] Act of March 2, 1793, c. 22, sec. 5, 1 Stat. 334; Rev. Stat., sec.
720; U.S.C.A., sec. 379; Jud. Code, sec. 265; Act of March 3, 1911, c.
231, sec. 265, 36 Stat. 1162.
[132] Diggs v. Wolcott (1807), 4 Cr. 179; Orton v. Smith (1856), 18
How. 263; Ex parte Sawyer (1888), 124 U.S. 200; Haines v. Carpenter
(1875), 91 U.S. 254; Dial v. Reynolds (1877), 96 U.S. 340; Chapman v.
Brewer (1885), 114 U.S. 158; U.S. v. Parkhurst-Davis Co. (1900),
176 U.S. 317; Hunt v. New York Cotton Exchange (1907), 205 U.S.
322; Hull v. Burr (1914), 234 U.S. 712; Essanay Film Mfg. Co. v. Kane

at the same time that the prohibition is not absolute and not without numerous exceptions. In the first place, in order to execute its judgments, to render its orders and decrees effectual, and protect jurisdiction that has been properly acquired, a federal court may enjoin proceedings in a state court which would defeat or impair its lawfully acquired jurisdiction.[133] Section 265 of the Judicial Code, then, is limited in its application by section 262, which empowers the federal courts "to issue all writs not specifically provided by statute, which may be necessary for the exercise of their respective jurisdictions, and agreeable to the principles and usages of law." [134] Under the strict supervision of the Supreme Court, this exercise of ancillary jurisdiction by the federal courts in the face of a statute to the contrary has not been a serious abuse of the statutory provisions. In the words of the Court the strict letter of the prohibition has been departed from, "while the spirit has been observed." [135] Moreover, in recent cases the Court has tended to contract the scope of this exception.[136]

(1922), 258 U.S. 358; Riehle v. Margolies (1929), 279 U.S. 218; Langnes v. Green (1931), 282 U.S. 531.

[133] Freeman v. Howe (1860), 24 How. 450; French v. Hay (1874), 22 Wall. 250; Dietzsch v. Huidekoper (1880), 103 U.S. 494; Ex parte Tyler (1893), 149 U.S. 164; Central National Bank v. Stevens (1898), 169 U.S. 432; Moran v. Sturges (1894), 154 U.S. 256; Harkrader v. Wadley (1898), 172 U.S. 148; Julian v. Central Trust Co. (1904), 193 U.S. 93; Madisonville Traction Co. v. St. Barnard Mining Co. (1905), 196 U.S. 239; Riverdale Cotton Mills v. Alabama & Georgia Mfg. Co. (1905), 198 U.S. 188; Hull v. Burr (1914), 234 U.S. 214; Chesapeake & Ohio R. Co. v. McCabe (1909), 213 U.S. 207.

[134] Kline v. Burke Construction Co. (1922), 260 U.S. 226, 229.

[135] Essanay Film Mfg. Co. v. Kane (1922), 258 U.S. 358.

[136] Langnes v. Green (1931), 282 U.S. 531; Riehle v. Margolies (1929), 279 U.S. 218; Essanay Film Mfg. Co. v. Kane (1922), 258 U.S. 358.

Two other exceptions to the prohibition from enjoining proceedings in state courts deserve notice. The first is that section 265 does not forbid a suit in the federal courts to stay the enforcement of a judgment or decree of a state court obtained by means of fraud or in circumstances that would render execution "contrary to recognized principles of equity and standards of good conscience."[137] The federal courts, however, cannot, by virtue of section 265 of the Judicial Code, restrain the execution of a judgment or decree of a state court because of mere irregularity.[138] Finally, the prohibition of section 265 of the Judicial Code does not prevent federal courts from enjoining the institution of suits or proceedings in state courts for the enforcement of state statutes or administrative orders which are repugnant to the Constitution of the United States and in which the elements of federal and equity jurisdiction are present.[139] In other words, an injunction restraining a party or potential party to a suit for the enforcement of an invalid statute is not a restraint against proceedings in a state court but an injunction against the wrongful acts of a private person.[140] The result of such an injunction, regardless of

---

[137] Wells Fargo and Co. v. Taylor (1920), 254 U.S. 175; Public Service Co. v. Corboy (1919), 250 U.S. 153; Ex parte Simon (1908), 208 U.S. 144; Marshall v. Holmes (1891), 141 U.S. 589; Gaines v. Fuentes (1875), 92 U.S. 10; Barrow v. Hunton (1878), 99 U.S. 80; Johnson v. Waters (1884), 111 U.S. 640; Arrowsmith v. Gleason (1889), 129 U.S. 86; Simon v. Southern Ry. Co. (1915), 236 U.S. 115; Robb v. Vos (1894), 155 U.S. 13.

[138] Marshall v. Holmes (1891), 141 U.S. 589; Ex parte Simon (1908), 208 U.S. 431; Simon v. Southern Ry. Co. (1915), 236 U.S. 115.

[139] Ex parte Young (1908), 209 U.S. 123; Truax v. Raich (1915), 239 U.S. 33; Missouri v. C.B. & Q. R. Co. (1916), 241 U.S. 533.

[140] Ex parte Young, *supra.*

such dialectics, is to prevent the state court from taking jurisdiction in such cases.

In none of the cases in which an exception has been made to the strict letter of the Act of 1793 has the Court intimated that the prohibition would be invalid if its terms were absolute and admitted of no exceptions. The statute has been construed as making the exceptions, and the constitutional issue has not arisen. As construed by the courts the terms of the statute are more severe than its application. Congress made one exception in terms; the Court has made three. Its total effect therefore has been slight. To quote Justice Sanford in a recent case:

> It is not a jurisdictional statute. It neither confers juris-
> diction upon the district courts nor takes away the jurisdic-
> tion, otherwise specifically conferred upon them by the
> Federal statutes. It merely limits their general equity powers
> in respect of the granting of a particular form of equitable
> relief; that is, it prevents from granting relief by way of
> injunction in the cases included within its inhibitions. In short
> it goes merely to the question of equity in the particular
> bill.[141]

Here, then, is an express admission on the part of the Supreme Court that in some cases, at least, Congress can withdraw from the courts the power to grant an injunction without otherwise increasing or diminishing their jurisdiction. The use of the ancillary writ of injunc-tion may, therefore, be regulated by Congress even in cases where equity jurisdiction exists. At least, that is the general tenor of the cases arising under section 265 of the Judicial Code.

[141] Smith v. Apple (1924), 264 U.S. 274, 278–279. See Hill v. Martin (1935), 296 U.S. 393, 403.

The judicial construction of those provisions of the Clayton Act regulating the use of the injunction in labor disputes presents a more difficult problem than the one just considered. The enormity of the economic interests involved, the emotional bias inherent in questions pertaining to industrial relations, and the struggle of opposing groups to manipulate the machinery of government in their own interests combine to present a far different picture from that presented in a prohibition to enjoin proceedings in state courts.

Section 20 of the Clayton Act granted private persons the right to sue for an injunction to restrain violations of the anti-trust acts, but provided at the same time that no injunction should be granted by a federal court in labor disputes "between employer and employees, or between employees, or between persons employed and persons selling employment . . . unless necessary to prevent irreparable injury to property, or to a property right, of the party making the application, for which injury there is no adequate remedy at law." Other provisions of the section prohibited injunctions against strikes and peaceful persuasion and legalized boycotts by peaceful persuasion and strike benefits.

In *Paine Lumber Co. v. Neal* [142] the Supreme Court construed these provisions as adding to the equity powers of the federal court and refused to grant the injunction sought by the lumber company because the acts complained of did not fall within the equity powers of the courts. Four years later in *Duplex Printing Co. v. Deering*,[143] the Court rejected this position and regarded the section as imposing "an exceptional and extraordinary

[142] (1917), 244 U.S. 459.   [143] (1921), 254 U.S. 493.

restriction upon the equity powers of the courts of the
United States, and upon the operation of the Anti-Trust
Laws—a restriction in the nature of a special privilege or
immunity to a particular class, with corresponding detri-
ment to the general public." [144] The section was, therefore, to be construed strictly. Accordingly, it was held
that the employer-employee relation had to be direct
and substantial. The terms "peaceful" and "lawful" were
given a narrow construction, and a secondary boycott
was regarded as not peaceful because "Congress had in
mind particular industrial controversies, not a general
class war." [145] But this was not the whole of the emasculation of the statute from the viewpoint of labor. The
opening paragraph of section 20 was construed as merely
putting in "statutory form familiar restrictions upon the
granting of injunctions already established and of general application in the equity practice of the courts of
the United States," and as "but declaratory of the law
as it stood before." [146]

Whatever the intention of Congress, no one will deny
that these provisions of the Clayton Act were given the
strictest possible construction in the *Duplex Printing Co.*
case. It and the cases that follow rendered the sections
of the act relating to the labor injunction a surplusage,
if not a nullity.[147] The intimations in *Truax v. Corrigan*
that due process of law requires a certain minimum of
protection in industrial disputes which neither Congress
nor the state legislatures may withhold and the strict
construction put upon the terms of the Clayton Act in

[144] *Ibid.*, 471–472.   [145] *Ibid.*, 472.   [146] *Ibid.*, 470.
[147] See also Bedford Cut Stone Co. v. Journeymen Stone Cutters'
Assoc. (1927), 274 U.S. 37; Industrial Association v. U.S. (1925), 268
U.S. 64; Michaelson v. U.S. (1924), 266 U.S. 42.

the *Duplex* case render any great curtailment of the equity powers of the federal courts of doubtful validity. Congress may deprive the courts of jurisdiction in suits between citizens of different states, and it may repeal section 20 of the Clayton Act, but this is an indirect way of correcting a specific evil. Moreover, as indicated by Professor Powell,[148] there still remains the *Debs* case [149] with the inherent power of the federal executive to go into the federal courts and seek an injunction against interference with the mails and the obstruction of interstate commerce.

Other examples of judicial emasculation of legislation designed to curb the judicial power are abundant. To provide for a more efficient administration of the revenue laws, Congress enacted a law in 1867 providing that "no suit for the purpose of restraining the assessment or collection of any tax shall be maintained in any court." [150] This provision later became section 3224 of the revised statutes, and it remains in the statute books today. The statute was enacted in pursuance of the inherent power of the government to protect itself against suits and under its right to prescribe the conditions under which it would subject itself to the process of its own courts in the collection of revenue.[151] In the exercise of this power Congress made a suit to recover taxes paid under protest the only remedy of the aggrieved taxpayer. For years this prohibition was strictly applied by the Supreme Court.[152] Although it had ruled in *Pollock v. Farmers'*

[148] *Op. cit.*, 13 Proc., Acad. Pol. Sci., 37, 73, 74.
[149] In re Debs (1895), 158 U.S. 564.   [150] 14 Stat. 475.
[151] Cheatham v. U.S. (1875), 92 U.S. 85.
[152] Snyder v. Marks (1883), 109 U.S. 189; Cheatham v. U.S. (1875), 92 U.S. 85; Shelton v. Platt (1891), 139 U.S. 591; Pacific Steam Whaling

Loan and Trust Co.[153] and *Brushaber v. Union Pacific Railroad Co.* [154] that the prohibition did not preclude a suit by a stockholder against a corporation to restrain the payment of a tax alleged to be unconstitutional where payment would result in confusion, wrong, multiplicity of suits, and the absence of all redress, the Court made no further inroads upon the absolute nature of the prohibition until 1916.

In *Dodge v. Osborn* [155] a bill to enjoin the assessment and collection of federal income taxes was dismissed by the Supreme Court of the District of Columbia. On appeal to the Supreme Court, counsel for appellant pressed the argument that section 3224 did not apply where, wholly independent of any allegation of unconstitutionality of the tax, additional equities and special or extraordinary circumstances were alleged, and that the right to an injunction in cases within the jurisdiction of a court of equity was a constitutional right which could not be destroyed or seriously impaired by an act of Congress. The Court held the suit to be within the terms of the prohibition and sustained the decree of the lower court. Chief Justice White, who spoke for the Court, however, did not stop here but went on to concede "for argu-

Co. v. U.S. (1903), 187 U.S. 447; Dodge v. Osborn (1916), 240 U.S. 118. The Supreme Court has been so reluctant to interfere with the collection of the revenues that with regard to state taxation it has formulated the rule that no suit to enjoin the assessment or collection of a state tax will be maintained on the mere ground of illegality. It must appear in addition that enforcement of the tax would lead to a multiplicity of suits or produce irreparable injury. Dows v. Chicago (1871), 11 Wall. 180; State Railroad Tax Cases (1875), 92 U.S. 575; Hannewinkle v. Georgetown (1872), 15 Wall. 548; Pittsburgh, Cincinnati & Chicago R. Co. v. Board of Public Works (1898), 172 U.S. 32.

[153] 157 U.S. 429; (1895), 158 U.S. 601.

[154] (1916), 240 U.S. 1.   [155] (1916), 240 U.S. 118.

ment's sake only" the contention that additional equities afforded a sufficient basis for the relief sought and to hold that the averments were insufficient.[156]

After the dismissal of the suit in *Dodge v. Osborn*, appellants filed a suit in a federal district court to enjoin the collection of surtaxes, alleging the same grounds in addition to the averment that they had filed with the collector an appeal or claim for the remission of surtaxes and that the commissioner had their protest under advisement. The preliminary injunction was denied, and on the same day a supplemental bill was filed alleging adverse action upon the taxpayer's protest and praying a recovery of the taxes paid under such protest. The District Court dismissed the suit on the merits. In cross appeals the Supreme Court sustained the action of the District Court in considering the merits of the case upon the ground that since the commissioner had considered all the questions involved and since the taxes had been paid, the case was "so exceptional in character as not to justify that . . . holding reversible error was committed by the court below, in passing upon the merits, thus putting an end to further and useless controversy." [157]

Chief Justice White's forensic proclivities that led him to make a generous concession "for argument's sake only" in *Dodge v. Osborn* and the action of the Court in sustaining the consideration of the merits of the case in *Dodge v. Brady* led to the complete emasculation of the prohibition against the maintenance of suits to enjoin the assessment or collection of taxes in the cases of *Hill v. Wallace* [158] and *Miller v. Standard Nut Margarine*

---

[156] *Ibid.*, 121.   [157] Dodge v. Brady (1916), 240 U.S. 122, 126.
[158] (1922), 259 U.S. 44.

Co.[159] In the former case a bill was filed to enjoin the collection of a tax on contracts for the sale of grain for future delivery as being a violation of due process law, the payment of which would result in a multiplicity of suits. On appeal the Supreme Court ruled that section 3224 did not "prevent an injunction in a case apparently within its terms in which some extraordinary and entirely exceptional circumstances make its provisions inapplicable," [160] and it held that the heavy penalties resulting from refusal to pay and the multiplicity of suits arising in case of payment were circumstances so extraordinary and exceptional as to render the prohibition inapplicable. Two reasons were suggested for this decision. The first was the combined effect of *Dodge v. Osborn* and *Dodge v. Brady*, which the Court used to justify its "exceptional circumstance" rule. The second was the fact that the Board of Trade and its directors were parties defendant, which brought the case within the rule of the *Pollock* and *Brushaber* cases.

The *Miller* case involved a suit to enjoin the collection of a tax on a nut product. No question of constitutionality was involved, but merely the issue of whether the product in question was taxable under the oleomargarine acts. On appeal the Supreme Court applied the rule enunciated in *Hill v. Wallace* and sustained the decree awarding the injunction. Section 3224 was held to be merely declaratory of the rule applied to state taxation that "where complainant shows that in addition to the illegality of an exaction in the guise of a tax there exist special and extraordinary circumstances, sufficient to bring the case within some acknowledged head of equity

[159] (1932), 284 U.S. 498.   [160] 259 U.S. 44, 62.

jurisprudence, a suit may be maintained to enjoin the collector." [161]

The full effects of judicial nullification of section 3224 of the revised statutes were not seen until the collection of processing taxes levied by the Agricultural Adjustment Act was almost stopped by injunctions in the lower federal courts. By October 1, 1935, more than sixteen hundred suits had been filed to restrain the collection of processing taxes.[162] Never in our history has the suspensory veto power of the inferior federal courts been more in evidence and more freely exercised. Following the rule in *Lipke v. Lederer* [163] to the effect that the statute did not forbid injunctions against the collection and penalties as distinguished from taxes and the principles asserted in the *Hill* and *Miller* cases, the lower federal courts encountered no difficulty in finding adequate grounds for ignoring the prohibition of section 3224 and the mandate of the Agricultural Adjustment Act.

Another act seemingly destined to judicial nullification is the Johnson Act of 1934,[164] which withdrew from the district courts jurisdiction "of any suit to enjoin, suspend, or restrain the enforcement, operation, or execution of any order of an administrative board or commission of a state," or any action in compliance with such an order

[161] 284 U.S. 498, 509. "The section," said Justice Butler, "does not refer specifically to the rule applicable to cases invoking exceptional circumstances. The general words employed are not sufficient, and it would require specific language undoubtedly disclosing that purpose, to warrant the inference that Congress intended to abrogate that salutary and well-established rule." P. 509.

[162] "Enjoining the Assessment and Collection of Federal Taxes Despite Statutory Prohibition" (1935), 49 Harv. L. Rev. 109. See also (1935), 3 U.S. Law Week 45.

[163] (1922), 259 U.S. 557.

[164] Act of May 14, 1934, c. 283, sec. 1, 48 Stat. 775.

"where jurisdiction is based solely upon the ground of diversity of citizenship, or the repugnance of such order to the Constitution of the United States, where such order (1) affects rates chargeable by a public utility, (2) does not interfere with interstate commerce, and (3) has been made after reasonable notice and hearing, and where a plain, speedy, and efficient remedy at law or in equity may be had in the courts of such state." That Congress hoped and intended to take away from the irresponsible power of the inferior federal courts to set aside rate regulations of state public service commissions and put an end to the almost interminable delays incidental to judicial usurpation of the rate-making function is amply proved by the hearings on the bill and the debate in Congress.[165] That Congress has failed to attain this result is equally well established by the attitude of the courts toward the act during the four years that have elapsed since its enactment.

The lower federal courts that have had occasion to apply the act have indicated that the requirements of "reasonable notice and hearing" in the statute contemplate a hearing within the meaning of "the fundamental requirements" of due process of law, that the state statutes must require reasonable notice and hearing rather than leave it to discretion or caprice,[166] and that the

[165] Jurisdiction of United States district courts over suits relating to orders of state administrative boards. House of Representatives, Committee on the Judiciary, Hearings on S. 752, 73rd Cong., 2nd Sess., 19th Sess., 1934. For the debate in the Senate see 78 Cong. Rec. 1915–1925, 2014–2024, 2027–2037, 2238–2243; see also the Senate Report on S. 152, 78 Cong. Rec. 2037–2048. For the House debate see 78 Cong. Rec. 8322–8351, 8415, 8416, 8432.

[166] Mississippi Power and Light Co. v. City of Jackson (1935), 9 Fed. Supp. 564.

utility company must know what evidence is to be considered against it.[167] The inferior courts have also ruled
that the requirements of a "plain, speedy and efficient
remedy at law or in equity" in the state courts contemplate judicial review as distinguished from legislative review,[168] thereby making the act inapplicable in those
states where the courts possess rate-making as well as
judicial functions. On appeal the Supreme Court concurred in this view, holding that the injunction should
have issued and that as long as the District Court was
doubtful of an effective judicial remedy in the state
courts, it should assume jurisdiction.[169]

In addition to sustaining this last principle applied by a
district court in the construction of the Johnson Act, the
Supreme Court has also added to the difficulties of its
application. In 1936 it reversed a district court's ruling
that a Montana statute prohibiting the issue of interlocutory decrees which restrained enforcement of the
commission's order until the determination of constitutional issues of confiscation raised by utilities companies did not preclude a plain, speedy, and efficient
remedy at law or in equity in the state courts.[170] The
Johnson Act was held not to apply because this state
statute "denying" a "plain, speedy, and efficient remedy
at law" had not been "authoritatively condemned" by

[167] Mississippi Power and Light Co. v. City of Aberdeen (1935),
11 Fed. Supp. 951.
[168] Georgia Continental Tel. Co. v. Georgia Public Service Commission (1934), 8 Fed. Supp. 434, 436; (1935), 9 Fed. Supp. 709.
[169] Corporation Commission of Oklahoma v. Cary (1935), 296 U.S.
452.
[170] Mountain States Power Co. v. Public Service Commission of
Montana (1936), 299 U.S. 167, 170, reversing Montana Power Co. v.
Public Service Commission (1935), 12 Fed. Supp. 746.

the state supreme court and because such a remedy could not "be predicated upon the problematical outcome of future consideration." [171] From this ruling it is but one short step to rulings in other cases involving statutory limitation of the use of the injunction to the effect that the inadequacy prerequisite to relief in a federal court is to be measured by the adequacy of the remedy afforded in federal and not state courts [172] and that the legal remedy must be as "practical and efficient to the ends of justice and its prompt administration, as the remedy in equity." [173] Added to this are the rules that such remedy must be judicial in character and the assumption that doubts of the adequacy of the judicial remedy shall be resolved in favor of the utility rather than the state courts.[174]

One apparent exception to the general trend toward judicial evisceration of statutes purporting to limit the power of courts deserves some notice. In general the Supreme Court has applied the restrictions of the Norris-La Guardia Act in good faith and has interpreted the law in conformity with the aims and purposes of Congress. Enacted in 1932 for the purpose of limiting the utility of the lower federal courts as strike-breaking agencies, this act provides that no court of the United States shall have jurisdiction to issue injunctions in labor disputes except after a hearing and findings to the effect that "un-

[171] *Supra,* 170.

[172] Di Giovanni v. Camden Fire Insurance Association (1935), 296 U.S. 64, 69. See also Henrietta Mills v. Rutherford County (1930), 281 U.S. 121; Smyth v. Ames (1898), 169 U.S. 466; Risty v. Chicago, Rock Island & Pacific R. Co. (1926), 270 U.S. 378.

[173] Boyce's Executors v. Grundy (1830), 3 Pet. 210, 215.

[174] Corporation Commission of Oklahoma v. Cary (1935), 296 U.S. 452.

lawful acts have been threatened and will be committed unless restrained or have been committed and will be continued unless restrained"; that substantial injury to the property of complainants will result; that as to the relief granted greater injury will be inflicted upon complainants by denying relief than will be inflicted upon defendants by granting it; that complainant has no adequate remedy at law; and that the public officers charged with the duty of protecting complainant's property are unable or unwilling to provide adequate protection to property. The act further defined a labor dispute so as to include "any controversy concerning terms or conditions of employment, or concerning the association or representation of the persons in negotiating, fixing, maintaining, changing, or seeking to arrange terms or conditions of employment regardless of whether or not the disputants stand in the proximate relation of employer and employee." [175]

That the act does not close all loopholes against the indiscriminate use of the injunction against employees in a labor dispute is evident from the exceptions contained in the act and from the definition of a labor dispute. Such exceptions are necessary in order to prevent constitutional questions from arising in the courts and to avoid outright invalidation. Once made they are usually extended by the courts, as demonstrated in the judicial history of the Johnson Act, the labor provisions of the Clayton Act, and section 265 of the Judicial Code. To the present, however, the Court has neither construed the act narrowly to avoid "serious constitutional ques-

[175] Act of March 23, 1932, 47 Stat. at L. 70.

tions," as in the *Michaelson* case, nor frittered away the act by seizing avidly upon its exceptions. Indeed, the Court has held the act to mean what it says.

In *Lauf v. E. G. Shinner and Company* [176] a suit had originally been brought by a Delaware corporation, which operated five meat markets in Milwaukee, in a district court to restrain a meat cutters' and butchers' union from picketing the places of business of the complainant because of complainant's refusal to establish and maintain a closed shop. The District Court made none of the findings required by the act save that of irreparable injury and the lack of an adequate remedy at law, but it ruled that no dispute as defined by the statute existed and accordingly issued the injunction against the union.

The Supreme Court held the District Court erred in the ruling that no labor dispute existed and in entering the decree without making the findings required by the act, and it reversed the holding of the Circuit Court of Appeals that this case did not come within prohibitions of the act because of the declarations of policy to the effect that employees are to have full freedom of association and designation of representatives free from restraint or coercion by employers, since the company could not accede to the union's demands in the face of the policy declared by Congress.

In *New Negro Alliance v. Sanitary Grocery Co.*[177] the controversy was even more remote from the employer-employee relationship, but again the Supreme Court reversed a district court by holding a labor dispute to exist and applying the act. The New Negro Alliance,

[176] (1938), 303 U.S. 323.   [177] (1938), 303 U.S. 552.

a charitable organization, had requested the company to adopt the policy of employing negro clerks in certain of its stores in the course of personnel changes. The company refused to do this. Then the alliance picketed one store, urging negroes to buy where they could work and threatening similar picketing of other stores. Although the picketing did not coerce customers, did not physically obstruct or harass persons entering the store, and was orderly, the district judge held the case did not involve a labor dispute, issued an injunction restraining the activities of the alliance, and was sustained in this action by the Court of Appeals of the District of Columbia on the ground that the dispute was a racial as distinguished from a labor dispute.

In reversing the lower courts, the Supreme Court, or rather Justice Roberts who spoke for the Court, manifested a conversance with history and legislative purposes so often absent from judicial opinions interpreting judicial power. The history of the act in Congress demonstrated to the Court that:

. . . it was the purpose of Congress further to extend the prohibitions of the Clayton Act respecting the exercise of jurisdiction by federal courts and to obviate the results of the judicial construction of that act. It was intended that peaceful and orderly dissemination of information by those defined as persons interested in labor disputes concerning "terms and conditions of employment" in an industry or a plant or a place of business should be lawful; that short of fraud, breach of the peace, violence, or conduct otherwise unlawful, those having a direct or indirect interest in such terms and conditions of employment should be at liberty to advertise and disseminate facts and information with respect to terms and conditions of employment, and peacefully to persuade others to concur in their views respecting an employer's practices.[178]

This far the only exceptions made by the Supreme Court to the operation of the Norris-La Guardia Act in addition to those found in the statute were made in *Virginian Ry. Co. v. System Federation*,[179] one of those unique cases in which an injunction was issued against an employer at the behest of employees in a labor dispute. The Supreme Court sustained a mandatory decree compelling the railway company to treat with the federation as the duly accredited representative of the shopcraft employees and restraining the railroad from influencing or coercing such employees in their free choice of representatives. The Court ruled that the injunction was not issued in defiance of section 9 of the act, which confines injunctions granted in labor disputes to "a prohibition of such specific act or acts as may be expressly complained of in the bill of complaint filed in such case and as shall be expressly included in . . . findings of fact made and filed by the court," and reasoned that the purpose of section 9 was not to preclude mandatory injunctions but "to forbid blanket injunctions which are usually prohibitory in form." Since the avowed purpose of the Norris-La Guardia Act was to free employees from interference, restraint, or coercion by employers in the choice of representatives or in the organization of employees for purposes of collective bargaining and internal aid and protection, the Norris-La Guardia Act was held to affect the decree only in so far as its provisions

[178] *Supra,* 562–563.   [179] (1937), 300 U.S. 515.

did not conflict with those of the amended Railway Labor Act.[180]

The enlightened interpretations of the Norris-La Guardia Act in the face of adverse decisions of the lower courts in the *Lauf, New Negro Alliance*, and other cases [181] may or may not be significant. Section 3224 of the revised statutes was applied scrupulously through a long period of years before being nullified almost overnight by the federal judiciary. Nevertheless, the decisions mark a definite departure from the previous emphasis upon the doctrine that Congress and state legislatures must afford a minimum of protection in order to meet the requirements of due process of law and its corollary, that legislation contracting such protection is to be construed strictly in order to avoid constitutional issues. Perhaps these decisions are but a reflection of an ephemeral attitude of a court chastened by a combination of election returns and a proposal to infuse it with a sufficient number of new members, a proposal that shocked the Court into what may be accurately called the Supreme Court revolution of 1938. If so, such atti-

---

[180] *Supra*, 562–563.

[181] See especially United Electric Coal Cos. v. Rice (C.C.A., 7th Cir., 1935), 80 F. (2nd) 1, where an injunction was sustained on the ground that the real controversy was between the United Mine Workers and the Progressive Mine Workers in which the coal company was not a party and that the act applied only to disputes between employers and employees; the Supreme Court denied certiorari (297 U.S. 714), but whether it approved the full opinion of the lower court is now immaterial in view of the rulings in the Lauf and Negro Alliance cases. See also Levering v. Garrigues (C.C.A., 2nd Cir., 1934), 71 F. (2nd) 284, where the Circuit Court upheld the act and reversed a decree of a district court defying the statute. See further Newton v. La Clede Steel Co. (C.C.A., 7th Cir.), 80 F. (2nd) 836, where a circuit court sustained a decree on the basis of some of the findings required by the act.

tude is probably destined to pass as soon as the lessons of chastisement are forgotten.

Nevertheless, the decisions of the Court in interpreting the Norris-La Guardia Act definitely demonstrate that it is not futile for Congress to enact and to re-enact legislation designed to overcome a negative and defeatist government by a judicial oligarchy acting under a system of equity that has been transformed into inequity. To enact and to re-enact legislation curbing the equity and certain alleged inherent powers of the federal courts is the only way in which Congress can limit what amounts to a claim of judicial prerogative. Congress has every right to press squarely upon the Court the so-called "serious constitutional questions" arising from congressional regulation of the judicial power and to attempt in every constitutional way to make the Court take the responsibility for its decisions construing such acts. The precise limits to the power of Congress to regulate, restrict, and control the jurisdiction and powers of the federal judiciary are not clearly delineated either in the Constitution or in judicial decisions. Congress, to preserve its own authority over a judiciary of its own creation, ought therefore to act aggressively upon the assumption that its power to establish inferior courts as it sees fit and to abolish them at will includes the lesser power of giving or withholding jurisdiction and powers at its discretion.[182] Judicial precedents, legislative practice, and political experience confirm this construction of congressional power. The basic assumptions of representative government and majority rule demand it.

[182] Stuart v. Laird (1803), 1 Cr. 299. See line of cases leading to Kline v. Burke Construction Co., 260 U.S. 226. *Supra.*

Chapter III

INCIDENTAL OR IMPLIED POWERS
OF FEDERAL COURTS

CLOSELY associated with the power of Congress to regulate the jurisdiction of courts of its own creation is the power to regulate and limit their incidental and implied powers. Such powers exist because of the belief that they inhere in judicial tribunals as an incident of their creation and existence as courts. Among such powers are included the power to punish for contempt, to adopt rules of procedure, to admit and disbar attorneys, to appoint masters in chancery and other necessary investigators, to prevent abuse of the judicial process, and to issue writs necessary for the exercise of jurisdiction. Some of these powers are expressly conferred upon courts by statute; others are subject to legislative regulation but not to destruction or abolition.[1] Although the Supreme Court has declared upon a number of occa-

[1] On the general subject of inherent court powers, see Leon Green, "The Court's Power over Admission and Disbarment" (1925), 4 Texas L. Rev. 1; E. R. Sunderland, "The Exercise of the Rule Making Power" (1926), 12 American Bar Assoc. Jour. 548; E. M. Morgan, "Judicial Regulation of Court Procedure" (1918), 2 Minn. L. Rev. 81; A. A. Bruce, "The Judicial Prerogative and Admission to the Bar" (1924), 19 Ill. L. Rev. 1; Felix Frankfurter and James Landis, "Power of Congress over Procedure in Criminal Contempts in 'Inferior' Federal Courts—A Study in Separation of Powers" (1924), 37 Harv. L. Rev. 1010.

sions that the powers of courts of the United States are conferred by act of Congress and cannot be extended beyond the powers thus conferred,[2] the tenacious persistence of the somewhat shadowy term "inherent powers" and the emphasis it has received in cases involving the incidental or implied powers of courts necessary to the efficient administration of justice, especially in cases involving the preservative power to punish contempts, create doubts concerning the power of Congress over the so-called inherent powers of courts.

Congress, it has been indicated in the two preceding chapters, cannot compel the courts of the United States to exercise jurisdiction in any case from which any essential elements of the judicial power have been abstracted. Among the essential elements of judicial power were noted such attributes as finality of judgment in a real and actual case or controversy, power to award execution, and freedom from interference in the decision of pending cases. Are there other essential elements of the judicial power of the United States? Do the so-called inherent powers of courts constitute indispensable attributes to the exercise of judicial power? If not, to what extent may Congress regulate or withhold such powers? Is it true that the Constitution makes a distinction between jurisdiction and judicial power to the effect that Congress can regulate the one but cannot control the other?

The answers to these questions depend not so much upon what the Supreme Court has said but upon what it and the inferior courts have done. This is best revealed

[2] U.S. v. Lawton (1847), 5 How. 10, 28; Assessor v. Osborne (1870), 9 Wall. 567, 575; Levy v. Fitzpatrick (1841), 15 Pet. 167, 171.

in judicial decisions and statutes pertaining to the power of courts to issue writs in aid of their jurisdiction, the incidental power of courts to make rules governing procedure, the necessary authority of courts of equity to appoint masters and other investigators, and finally the self-preserving power of courts to punish contempts of their authority.

Acting upon the theory that a statutory grant of power was necessary if courts were to have authority to issue writs in aid of their jurisdiction, the First Congress empowered courts of the United States "to issue writs of *scire facias, habeas corpus* and all other writs not specially provided for by statute, which may be necessary for the exercise of their respective jurisdictions, and agreeable to the principles and usages of law." [3] This provision, it should be noted, conferred no general power to issue writs but limited such power to issuance in aid of jurisdiction.

In *McIntire v. Wood* [4] plaintiff had sought a writ of mandamus directing the register of a land office to issue a final certificate of purchase. The eleventh section of the original judiciary act conferred jurisdiction upon the circuit courts in all diversity cases of a civil nature at the common law or in equity where the matter in dispute exceeded five hundred dollars, but it failed to confer upon such courts jurisdiction in cases arising under the Constitution and laws of the United States. Upon a certificate of division of opinion from the Circuit Court of Ohio, the Supreme Court ruled that the lower tribunal had no power to issue the writ of mandamus since its

[3] Judiciary Act of 1789, 1 Stat. at L. 81, 82.
[4] (1813), 7 Cr. 504.

power to issue such writs was confined exclusively to those cases in which the writ was necessary to the exercise of their jurisdiction.

Eight years later a case involving the same state of facts, with the exception that the parties were entitled to bring suit in the federal courts under the eleventh section of the Judiciary Act, again arose in the Circuit Court for Ohio. The Supreme Court applied the rule enunciated in *McIntire v. Wood* and held that the circuit courts could issue writs of mandamus only "in cases where the jurisdiction already exists and not where it is to be courted or acquired, by means of the writ proposed to be sued out." [5]

Not until *Kendall v. United States* [6] was a suitor able to obtain a mandamus against an officer of the United States compelling him to perform a ministerial duty. In this case the suit had been brought originally in the United States Circuit Court for the District of Columbia. On a writ of error the Supreme Court of the United States sustained the power of the lower court to issue the writ in question on the ground that it was a common-law court with the powers of a court of general jurisdiction, among which was the power to issue prerogative writs.

The result of these three cases is that the courts of the United States, being of limited jurisdiction, have no general inherent power to issue prerogative writs but derive such power solely from statute. Since the statute limits the exercise of this power to cases in aid of jurisdiction already acquired, the inferior federal courts have

[5] McClung v. Silliman (1821), 6 Wh. 598, 601, 602.
[6] (1838), 12 Pet. 524.

no power to grant mandamus in an independent or original proceeding.[7]

What is true of mandamus is generally true of the remedial writ of habeas corpus. In 1807 in *Ex parte Bollman* Chief Justice Marshall proclaimed that the power to award a writ of habeas corpus had to be conferred by written law. In his denial of any common-law jurisdiction of the federal courts, however, he was careful to indicate that this was not to be considered as abridging the power of the courts over their own officers or to protect themselves and their members from being disturbed in the exercise of their functions.[8] To the same effect is *Ex parte Yerger*[9] in which the petitioner was held in the custody of the military authorities in Mississippi. Referring to the prohibition against the suspension of the writ of habeas corpus, the Court plainly inferred that Congress is not bound to provide for the protection of federal rights by investing the Court of the United States with jurisdiction to protect those rights.[10]

The result of these cases is that the power to issue prerogative and other writs is purely statutory and cannot be extended beyond the statutory grant.[11] Like the

[7] Knox County v. Aspinwall (1861), 24 How. 376; Amy v. Supervisors (1871), 11 Wall. 136; Bath County v. Amy (1872), 13 Wall. 244; Secretary v. McGarrahan (1870), 9 Wall. 298; Graham v. Norton (1873), 15 Wall. 427; Heine v. Board of Levee Commissioners (1874), 19 Wall. 655; Louisiana v. Jumel (1883), 107 U.S. 711; Davenport v. County of Dodge (1882), 105 U.S. 237; Smith v. Bourbon County (1888), 127 U.S. 105.

[8] 4 Cr. 75, 93, 94.   [9] (1869), 8 Wall. 85.

[10] For further discussion of the power of the federal courts in habeas corpus cases see Ex p. Royall (1886), 117 U.S. 241; Frank v. Mangum (1915), 237 U.S. 309.

[11] For further interpretations of the power of Congress to issue writs, see McClellan v. Carland (1910), 217 U.S. 268; In re Massachu-

writ of mandamus, the writ of injunction is an auxiliary writ and can be used only in the exercise of jurisdiction previously required. Assuming, then, that there exists a distinction between jurisdiction and judicial power which permits Congress to regulate the one but forbids it to restrict the other, Congress can prevent the issuance of injunctions by withholding jurisdiction from the courts in general classes of cases. Thus, if Congress should withdraw from the federal courts jurisdiction in all cases involving a federal question, they would have no power to enjoin the enforcement of a statute because of repugnancy to the Constitution.

The power of Congress to restrict the use of the injunction in cases where the courts have jurisdiction presents a more serious problem, but here again the weight of precedent is on the side of congressional authority. Congress has restricted the use of the injunction to restrain proceedings in state courts, to restrain the assessment and collection of taxes, and to enjoin acts of labor in industrial disputes. Finally, Congress has provided a statutory court of three judges for the hearing of injunction suits arising under the Interstate Commerce Act and suits in which it is sought to restrain the enforcement of state statutes on the ground of unconstitutionality. All of these acts relate to the particular use of the injunction in cases where the courts have jurisdiction. Although it

---

setts (1905), 197 U.S. 482; Fink v. O'Neil (1882), 106 U.S. 272; Ex p. Milwaukee R. Co. (1867), 5 Wall. 188; Wayman v. Southard (1825), 10 Wh. 1; U.S. Bank v. Halstead (1825), 10 Wh. 51; In re Claasen (1891), 140 U.S. 200; Goddard v. Ordway (1877), 94 U.S. 672; Hardeman v. Anderson (1846), 4 How. 640; U.S. v. Beatty (1914), 232 U.S. 463; U.S. v. Dickinson (1909), 213 U.S. 92; Whitney v. Dick (1906), 202 U.S. 132; In re Chetwood (1897), 165 U.S. 443.

is true that some of them have been eviscerated by judicial decisions, all of them have, at one time or another, been applied and sustained as a valid exercise of congressional power.

The power to issue writs, therefore, is a statutory power and may, therefore, be expanded or restricted by statute. Whether Congress can totally destroy this power and still compel the courts to exercise jurisdiction is doubtful. Regulation is valid, however, so long as Congress does not impede the efficient exercise of the judicial power or impair the essential independence of the courts. What these limits are is a question for judicial determination. Thus the right of the courts to define the limits of legislative power carries with it the power of courts to determine their own powers.

The power of courts to issue writs and other process does not cease with the mere determination of the case and the adjudication of the issues before it, because jurisdiction is not exhausted by mere rendition of judgment but continues until such judgment or decree is executed.[12] Consequently, process subsequent to judgment is as essential to jurisdiction as process antecedent to judgment, or else, as Justice Clifford expressed it, "the judicial power would be incomplete and entirely inade-

[12] Wayman v. Southard (1825), 10 Wh. 1, 23; Riggs v. Johnson County (1867), 6 Wall. 166, 187. See also Walker v. Powers (1882), 104 U.S. 245; Central Nat. Bank v. Stevens (1898), 169 U.S. 432; Mills v. Duryee (1813), 7 Cr. 481; Supreme Tribe of Ben-Hur v. Cauble (1921), 255 U.S. 356; Murphy v. John Hofman Co. (1909), 211 U.S. 562; Raphael v. Trask (1904), 194 U.S. 272; Riverdale Cotton Mills v. Ala. & Ga. Mfg. Co. (1905), 198 U.S. 188; Byers v. McAuley (1893), 149 U.S. 608; Rickey Land and Cattle Co. v. Miller (1910), 218 U.S. 258; Eichel v. U.S. Fidelity & Guaranty Co. (1917), 245 U.S. 102; United Fuel Gas Co. v. R.R. Commission (1929), 278 U.S. 300. Compare Virginia v. West Virginia (1918), 246 U.S. 565.

quate to the purposes for which it was conferred by
the Constitution." [13] Accordingly, after judgment has
been rendered, courts have ancillary jurisdiction to issue
ancillary writs and process of execution for the purpose
of enforcing such judgment.

Although judicial power essentially involves the right
to enforce the results of its exertion and jurisdiction [14]
and an award of execution is a part and an essential part
of every judgment, the power to award execution is
derived from legislative enactments.[15] Congress, therefore, possesses "the uncontrolled power to legislate in
respect both to the form and effect of execution and
other final process to be issued in the Federal Courts." [16]
This rule was first enunciated by Chief Justice Marshall
in the case of *Wayman v. Southard* [17] and has been applied ever since. In *Fink v. O'Neil* [18] in which the government of the United States attempted to enforce by
summary process the payment of a debtor, the Supreme
Court held that under the process acts law of Wisconsin
was the law of the United States and that, therefore, the
government was required to bring a suit, obtain a judgment, and cause execution to issue. "The courts," said
Justice Matthews, speaking for a unanimous court, "have
no inherent authority to take any one of these steps, except as it may have been conferred by the legislative de-

[13] Riggs v. Johnson County (1867), 6 Wall. 166, 187. See also the
cases cited in the preceding notes.

[14] Wayman v. Southard (1825), 10 Wh. 1; and the cases cited in n. 12.

[15] Gordon v. U.S. (1864), 117 U.S. app. 697; Muskrat v. U.S. (1911),
219 U.S. 346.

[16] Riggs v. Johnson County (1867), 6 Wall. 166, 187–188.

[17] (1825), 10 Wh. 1. See also U.S. Bank v. Halstead (1825), 10 Wh. 51.

[18] (1882), 106 U.S. 272, 280.

partment; for they can exercise no jurisdiction, except as the law confers and limits it."

Among the powers commonly deemed to inhere in courts of justice is the power to make all necessary rules for governing their process and practice and for the orderly conduct of their business. The power of courts to frame reasonable and necessary rules, however, is limited by statute and cannot go beyond it.[19] The leading case is *Wayman v. Southard*,[20] which involved the validity of the process acts of 1789 and 1792, making the rules governing the forms of writs the same in each state as were used by the highest court in each state, subject to such alterations as the federal courts or the Supreme Court might deem expedient.[21]

In answer to contention of counsel that Congress could not delegate to the courts the legislative power of making rules governing process and execution, Chief Justice Marshall assumed that the power was legislative in nature and replied that it was merely a power to vary minor regulations "within the great outlines marked out by the legislature in directing the execution." Because of the necessary and proper clause, Marshall entertained no doubts as to the power of Congress over the subject.[22] As stated by Justice Thompson in a case involving the application of the same acts:

[19] Hecker v. Fowler (1864), 2 Wall. 123; In re Hien (1897), 166 U.S. 432; Washington–Southern Navigation Co. v. Baltimore & P.S.B. Co. (1924), 263 U.S. 629.

[20] (1825), 10 Wh. 1.

[21] Act of Sept. 29, 1789, c. 21, 1 Stat. at L. 93; Act of May 8, 1792, c. 36, 1 Stat. at L. 275.

[22] 10 Wh. 1, 22. In U.S. Bank v. Halstead (1825), 10 Wh. 51, 53, involving a similar situation and the validity of the same statutes, Justice Thompson stated:

The authority to carry into complete effect the judgments of the courts necessarily results, by implication, from the power to ordain and establish such courts. But it does not rest altogether upon such implication; for express authority is given to Congress to make all laws which shall be necessary and proper for carrying into execution all the powers vested by the Constitution in the government of the United States, or in any department or officer thereof. The right of Congress, therefore, to regulate the proceedings on executions, and direct the mode and manner . . . is not to be questioned.[23]

Although the principal function of court rules is to regulate the practice of the Court with regard to the forms, the operation and effect of process, and the mode and times for proceedings, sometimes rules are employed to state in convenient form "a principle of substantive law which has been established by statute or decisions."

"It cannot certainly be contended, with the least color of plausibility, that Congress does not possess the uncontrolled power to legislate with respect both to the form and effect of executions issued upon judgments recovered in the courts of the United States. The judicial power would be incomplete, and entirely inadequate to the purposes for which it was intended, if, after judgment, it could be arrested in its progress, and denied the right of enforcing satisfaction in any manner which shall be prescribed by the laws of the United States."

The element common to the Southard and Halstead cases is the conflict between federal and state authority. To uphold the authority of the federal government and its courts, it was necessary first to sustain congressional power. Thus a rule originally enunciated to justify the federal judicial power has come to sustain the power of Congress in any conflict between legislative and judicial authority in the national government.

[23] U.S. Bank v. Halstead, *supra*, 53–54. The discretionary power of the federal courts under the Act of 1793 was restricted by the Act of May 19, 1828, c. 68, 4 Stat. at L. 278. This act was sustained and applied in Fink v. O'Neil (1882), 106 U.S. 272. With regard to process, then, Congress can make the rules governing it and delegate that power to the courts or to the legislatures or courts of the states. See also Beers v. Haughton (1835), 9 Pet. 329.

No rule of court, however, "can enlarge or restrict jurisdiction. Nor can a rule abrogate or modify the substantive law. This is true, whether the court to which the rules apply be one of law, of equity, or of admiralty. It is true of rules of practice prescribed by this court for inferior tribunals, as it is of those rules which lower courts make for their own guidance under authority conferred." [24]

A court likewise has the inherent power to supervise the conduct of its officers, parties, witnesses, counsel, and jurors in a case by its own self-preserving rules for the protection of rights of litigants and the orderly administration of justice.[25] Similarly, there is inherent in the federal courts the power to amend these records, correct the mistakes of the clerk or other officer of court, and to supply defects or omissions in their records even after the lapse of a term.[26] But the power to amend its records gives a court no power to create a record or to re-create one of which no evidence exists.[27]

Courts of justice also possess inherent equitable powers

[24] Washington–Southern Navigation Co. v. Baltimore and P.S.B. Co. (1924), 263 U.S. 629, 635–636; Ward v. Chamberlain (1863), 2 Bl. 430, 435–437; Hudson v. Parker (1895), 156 U.S. 277, 284; Venner v. Great Northern R. Co. (1908), 209 U.S. 24, 33–34; Davidson Marble Co. v. U.S. (1909), 213 U.S. 10, 18; Mills v. Bank of U.S. (1826), 11 Wh. 431, 439–440; Patterson v. Winn (1831), 5 Pet. 233, 243; The St. Lawrence (1862), 1 Bl. 522, 530; Manhattan Life Insurance Co. v. Francisco (1873), 17 Wall. 672, 679; The Lottawanna (1875), 21 Wall. 558, 579; The Corsair (1892), 145 U.S. 335, 342.

[25] Griffin v. Thompson (1844), 2 How. 244, 257; McDonald v. Pless (1915), 238 U.S. 264, 266.

[26] Gagnon v. U.S. (1904), 193 U.S. 451; In re Wight (1890), 134 U.S. 136; Gonzales v. Cunningham (1896), 164 U.S. 612; U.S. v. Vigil (1870), 10 Wall. 423. This power was conferred by the revised statutes.

[27] Gagnon v. U.S., *supra*, 458.

over their own process to prevent abuse, oppression, and injustice, and to protect their own jurisdiction and officers in the protection of property in the custody of law.[28] Such a power "is essential to and is inherent in the organization of courts of justice." [29]

The administration of insolvent enterprises, investigations into the reasonableness of rates, and the performance of many of the equity functions of a court require the appointment of masters in chancery, referees, and other investigators. In *Hecker v. Fowler* [30] the practice of referring pending actions to a referee was held to be coeval with the organization of federal courts and as fully warranted by law as trial by jury.[31]

Ex parte Peterson [32] is the leading case. In an action at law by a receiver to collect a balance alleged to be due, the United States district judge appointed an auditor with power to compel the attendance of witnesses and the production of testimony and authorized him to make a preliminary investigation of the facts and to file a report thereon for the purpose of simplifying the issues for the jury. The auditor was further authorized to form a judgment and express an opinion upon the matters in dispute without, however, making any final decisions.

No statute authorized this action, but, on the other

[28] Gumbel v. Pitkin (1888), 124 U.S. 131; Krippendorf v. Hyde (1884), 110 U.S. 276, 283; Buck v. Colbath (1865), 3 Wall. 334; Hagan v. Lucas (1836), 10 Pet. 400; Covell v. Heyman (1884), 111 U.S. 176.

[29] Eberly v. Moore (1861), 24 How. 147, 158; Arkadelphia Milling Co. v. St. Louis S.W.R. Co. (1919), 249 U.S. 134.

[30] (1864), 2 Wall. 123.

[31] *Ibid.*, 128–129. Citing York and Cumberland R. Co. v. Myers (1855), 18 How. 246; Thornton v. Carson (1813), 7 Cr. 596; Carnochan v. Christie (1826), 11 Wh. 446; Luts v. Linthicum (1834), 8 Pet. 165.

[32] (1920), 253 U.S. 300.

hand, none prohibited it either directly or by implication. "Courts," declared Justice Brandeis, "have (at least,
in the absence of legislation to the contrary) inherent
power to provide themselves with appropriate instruments required for the performance of their duties. . . .
This power includes authority to appoint persons un-
connected with the court to aid judges in the performance of specific judicial duties, as they may arise in the
progress of a cause." [33]

The power to appoint auditors has been exercised by
the federal courts sitting in equity since their very beginning,[34] but the inherent power of a federal court to
invoke such assistance is the same whether the Court
sits at law or in equity.[35] In the *Peterson* case the judge
was held to require the aid of an auditor because, "without the aid to be rendered through the preliminary hearing and report, the trial judge would be unable to perform his duty of defining to the jury the issues submitted
for their determination, and of directing their attention
to the matters actually in issue." [36]

In 1916 the power of the federal courts to suspend
sentence in criminal cases without authorization by statute was denied by the Supreme Court in *Ex parte
United States*.[37] Chief Justice White, who spoke for the
Court, admitted that the trial of offenses and the imposi-

[33] *Ibid.*, 312.   [34] Kimberly v. Arms (1889), 129 U.S. 512, 523.
[35] Ex p. Peterson (1920), 253 U.S. 300, 314; Hecker v. Fowler (1864),
2 Wall. 123.
[36] Ex p. Peterson, 253 U.S. 300, 313–314. A compulsory reference to
an auditor with power finally to determine issues is impossible in the
federal courts because of the guaranty of trial by jury in action at law.
For the functions of auditors in such cases see Field v. Holland (1810),
6 Cr. 8, 21; North Carolina R. Co. v. Swasey (1875), 23 Wall. 405, 410.
[37] (1916), 242 U.S. 27.

tion of punishment upon conviction were judicial in nature and that in performing these functions courts inherently possessed "ample right to exercise reasonable,
that is, judicial discretion to enable them to wisely exert
their authority." Nevertheless, this did not mean that
courts might suspend sentence without the authorization
of statute. The exercise of such a power, reasoned the
Chief Justice, rested upon the proposition "that the
power to enforce begets inherently a discretion to perma-
nently refuse to do so." [38]

Of the inherent powers of courts considered thus far,
none, with the solitary exception of the power to issue
writs, is absolutely essential to the independent exercise
of the judicial power or indispensable to the self-preservation and existence of the courts. Consequently, it may
be expected that the regulatory power of Congress as it
relates to such powers is largely a matter of discretion.
Such powers are presumed to exist in the absence of a
statute, but at no time is it indicated that they would exist
in the face of a statutory prohibition. The power of
courts to issue writs of mandamus, execution, and habeas
corpus and the extent of congressional authority to restrict the issuance of such writs were settled in favor of
legislative discretion at an early time in our constitutional
law when the great constitutional issues took the form of
conflicts between state and national authority rather
than between legislative and judicial power. As a consequence only the power of Congress to limit the use of
the injunction remains doubtful.

Of all the so-called inherent powers of courts none is
quite so important and none so subject to abuse as the

[38] *Ibid.,* 41–42.

power to punish contempts. As the most efficient instrument in the enforcement of judicial orders and decrees, it supplements and complements the injunction, and the two exercised indiscriminately may become twin instruments of judicial oppression. On the other hand, such a power is requisite to the self-preservation of courts and to the vindication of judicial authority. Justice Lamar summarized the attitude of the courts well in *Gompers v. Buck's Stove and Range Co.*[39] when he said:

> For while it is sparingly to be used, yet the power of courts to punish for contempts is a necessary and integral part of the independence of the judiciary, and is absolutely essential to the performance of the duties imposed on them by law. Without it they are mere boards of arbitration whose judgments and decrees would be only advisory.

The assertion of what amounts to a prerogative on the part of courts to punish for contempt began in 1765 in Great Britain in the case of *Rex v. Almon*[40] when Justice Wilmot in an unofficial opinion declared:

> The principle upon which attachments are granted in respect of bailiffs is to facilitate the execution of the law by giving a summary and immediate redress and protection to the persons who undertake it. . . . But the principle upon which attachments issue for libels upon the courts is of a more enlarged and important nature—it is to keep a blaze of glory around them and to deter people from attempting to render them contemptible in the eyes of the public.[41]

The contempt power of the courts has its roots in English law, but its growth and development in the

[39] (1911), 221 U.S. 418, 450.
[40] *Wilmot's Notes*, 243; John Charles Fox, "The King v. Almon" (1908), 24 Law Quarterly Rev. 184, 266.
[41] Quoted by Fox, *ibid.*, 197.

United States is indigenous to a soil made fertile by a written constitution, the doctrine of the separation of powers, and judicial review. Accordingly, the power of the courts of the United States is partly a historical product of English practice and partly a deviation from historical growth because of the legal and political peculiarities of the American constitutional system.

In some very able researches Mr. John Charles Fox has traced the development of the power of English courts to punish by summary process contempts of their authority.[42] As a result of his studies, Mr. Fox thinks that commitment for contempt may have originated in the Statute of Westminster (13 Edward I, c. 39), which provided punishment by imprisonment for resistance to the King's precepts, or in the power of Parliament as the highest court of the realm to punish contempts of its authority.[43] At any rate it is certain that disobedience of court orders under Norman and later under English law was regarded as contempt of the King himself and that attachment was a prerogative process derived from presumed contempt of the sovereign.[44] It is also certain that at one time a jury was summoned to try contumelious contempts [45] and that no instance has been found earlier

---

[42] "The King v. Almon," *supra;* "The Summary Process to Punish Contempt" (1909), 25 Law Qu. Rev. 238, 354; "Criminal Contempt" (1914), 30 Law Qu. Rev. 56; "Eccentricities of the Law of Contempt of Court" (1920), 36 Law Qu. Rev. 394; "The Practice in Contempt of Court Cases" (1922), 38 Law Qu. Rev. 185.

[43] "The King v. Almon," *supra,* 192, 276.

[44] *Ibid.,* 194–195. See the opinion of Fletcher, J., in Taafe v. Downes (1813), 3 Moo. P.C. 36; 50 R.R. 14.

[45] "The King v. Almon," *supra,* 184, 196; see also Lord Hale's "Discourse Concerning the Courts of King's Bench and Common Pleas," *Hargrave's Tracts,* 363.

than 1720 of a proceeding for libel upon a court other than by indictment, information, or action at law.

Down to the fifteenth century some criminal contempts were tried by criminal or quasi-criminal process in the ordinary course of the law.[46] In the latter part of the seventeenth century, criminal contempts committed altogether outside of court by persons other than officers of the Court were punished according to ordinary legal procedure.[47] A century later Blackstone regarded immemorial usage as the basis for the punishment of all kinds of contempt by summary process of attachment,[48] and in the same century summary power was extended to all contempts whether committed in or out of court.[49]

---

[46] "The King v. Almon," *supra*, 277; "The Summary Process to Punish Contempt," *supra*, 244.

[47] *Ibid.*, 246.   [48] *Ibid.*, 247, citing 4 Bl. Com., c. 20, sec. 3.

[49] *Ibid.*, 252. The results of Fox's researches are summarized in "The King v. Almon," *supra*, at pp. 276–277 as follows:

"Originally the superior courts of common law had jurisdiction to punish disobedience to the King's writ summarily by fine and imprisonment upon attachment, and probably also a disciplinary jurisdiction over their own officers exercisable summarily. The Court of King's Bench had jurisdiction on indictment or bill to punish contempts *in facie*, obstructions to the service of process, other obstructions to the administration of justice as by libeling the court or a judge or assaulting a party on his way to the court, and deceit or collusion in connection with pending proceedings. In later times—perhaps in or after the Tudor period—the common law courts gradually established a summary jurisdiction over most of those contempts which had been formerly the subject of indictment or bill, but this did not extend to libels on the court or judges which were still punished by indictment or by proceedings in the Star Chamber, and upon the abolition of that court, by information or indictment in the King's Bench. The Council, or the Star Chamber as representing the Council, had always exercised a concurrent jurisdiction to punish contempts of other Courts, and as the Star Chamber Records show, had exercised it largely. Upon the abolition of that Court a large portion of its jurisdiction devolved upon the King's Bench, and libels, including libels

The summary power of courts to punish contempts, therefore, is not a power derived from immemorial usage but a power seized upon and developed by the courts themselves.

Section 17 of the Judiciary Act of 1789 provided that all courts of the United States should have "power . . . to punish by fine or imprisonment, at the discretion of said courts, all contempts of authority in any case or hearing before the same." The only limitation placed upon this blanket grant of discretion was that it was made "a negation of all other modes of punishment." [50] The injudicious use of this broad grant of power led to impeachment proceedings against Judge James H. Peck of the Federal District Court for the District of Missouri and to the enactment of a law in 1831 restricting the powers of the federal courts to punish contempts.[51]

---

upon Courts and judges, were punished by information or indictment down to the early part of the eighteenth century."

[50] Ex p. Robinson (1874), 19 Wall. 505, 512.

[51] For a summary of the Peck impeachment trial and the circumstances leading to the Act of 1831, see the excellent article by Professors Frankfurter and Landis, "Power of Congress over Procedure in Criminal Contempts in 'Inferior' Federal Courts—A Study in Separation of Powers" (1924), 37 Harv. L. Rev. 1010, 1024–1028. For a complete report of the trial, see Stansbury, *Report of the Trial of James H. Peck* (Boston, 1833). Prior to the Peck impeachment Justice Story had recognized in Ex p. Kearney (1822), 7 Wh. 38, 45, that such a power may be subject to abuse "which will be a public grievance, for which a remedy may be applied by the legislature." In no case before 1831 did the Court suggest that Congress could not regulate the power to punish contempts. In United States v. Hudson and Goodwin (1812), 7 Cr. 32, 34, the Supreme Court held that the federal courts had no common-law jurisdiction and no implied power to punish libels against the President and the Congress of the United States, but it went on to speak of the power to fine and imprison for contempt and to enforce the observance of order as powers "which cannot be dispensed with in a court, because they are necessary to the exercise of all others."

The Act of March 2, 1831, limited the power of the federal courts to punish contempts by summary attachment to misbehavior of persons in the presence of the Court, "or so near thereto as to obstruct the administration of justice";[52] to the misbehavior of officers of the Court in their official capacity; and to disobedience or resistance to any lawful writ, process, or order of the Court. Attempts to obstruct the administration of justice by intimidation were made punishable by fine or imprisonment upon indictment and conviction.

The act was applied in good faith by the lower federal courts,[53] and in 1873, forty-two years after its enactment, its validity was sustained by the Supreme Court in *Ex parte Robinson*.[54] Here a witness, upon the advice of

[52] C. 99, 4 Stat. at L. 487; now Jud. Code, sec. 268. The text of the statute follows:

"*Be it enacted* . . . that the power of the several courts of the United States to issue attachments, and inflict summary punishments for contempts of court, shall not be construed to extend to any cases except the misbehaviour of any person or persons in the presence of the said courts, or so near thereto as to obstruct the administration of justice, the misbehaviour of any of the officers of the said courts in their official transactions, and the disobedience or resistance by any officer of the said courts, party, juror, witness, or any other person or persons, to any lawful writ, process, order, rule, decree, or command of the said courts.

"Sec. 2. *And be it further enacted*, that if any person or persons shall, corruptly, or by threats or force, endeavor to influence, intimidate, or impede any juror, witness, or officer, in any court of the United States, in the discharge of his duty, or shall, corruptly, or by threats or force, obstruct, or impede, or endeavor to obstruct or impede, the due administration of justice therein, every person or persons, so offending shall be liable to prosecution therefor, by indictment, and shall, on conviction thereof, be punished, by fine not exceeding five hundred dollars, or by imprisonment, not exceeding three months, or both, according to the nature and aggravation of the offence."

[53] Ex p. Poulson (1835), 19 Fed. Case No. 11,350, p. 1205; U.S. v. Holmes (1842), 26 Fed. Case No. 15,383, pp. 360, 363.

[54] (1874), 19 Wall. 505.

Robinson, an attorney, had suddenly absented himself from court. The United States District Court for the District of Arkansas ordered Robinson and others to appear and show cause why they should not be punished for contempt of court. Robinson refused to answer and was disbarred upon the order of the judge. Upon application for a writ of mandamus, the Supreme Court directed that the order of disbarment be vacated because no act of Robinson could be construed as contempt of court under the Act of 1831.

Justice Field, who spoke for the Court, said:

The power to punish for contempts is inherent in all courts; its existence is essential to the preservation of order in judicial proceedings, and to the enforcement of the judgments, orders, and writs of the courts, and consequently to the due administration of justice. The moment the courts of the United States were called into existence and invested with jurisdiction over any subject, they became possessed of this power. But the power has been limited and defined by the act of Congress of March 2, 1831. The act, in terms, applies to all courts; whether it can be held to limit the authority of the Supreme Court, which derives its existence and powers from the Constitution, may perhaps be a matter of doubt. But that it applies to the Circuit and District Courts there can be no question. These courts were created by an act of Congress. Their powers and duties depend upon the act calling them into existence, or subsequent acts extending or limiting their jurisdiction.[55]

The excerpt quoted above contained a serious contradiction although Justice Field went on to state that the summary powers of the inferior federal courts to punish for contempts could, under the act, "only be exercised to

[55] *Ibid.*, 510–511.

insure order and decorum in their presence, to secure
faithfulness on the part of their officers in their official
transaction, and to enforce obedience to their lawful
orders, judgments, and processes," and then to give the
act its fullest application. Powers inherent in a court
merely by virtue of its creation and existence can hardly
be reconciled with the powers of Congress asserted by
Justice Field.

In time the emphasis placed upon the inherent power
of courts to punish for contempt came to overshadow
the authority of Congress to regulate or restrict the jurisdiction and powers of courts of its own creation.[56] Although the Supreme Court continued to regard the Act
of 1831 as a restriction upon summary punishments for
contempt,[57] after 1890 it began to express doubts con-

[56] See Ex p. Terry (1888), 128 U.S. 289. In re Savin (1889), 131 U.S.
267; Eilenbecker v. District Court of Plymouth County (1890), 134
U.S. 31; In re Debs (1895), 158 U.S. 564; Interstate Commerce Commission v. Brimson (1894), 154 U.S. 447; Bessette v. W. B. Conkey Co.
(1904), 194 U.S. 324; Gompers v. Buck's Stove and Range Co. (1911),
221 U.S. 418. See also Anderson v. Dunn (1821), 6 Wh. 204; In re Del-
gado (1891), 140 U.S. 586; Toledo Scale Co. v. Computing Scale Co.
(1923), 261 U.S. 399; Ex p. Hudgings (1919), 249 U.S. 378; Doyle v.
London Guarantee and Accident Co. (1907), 204 U.S. 599; Ex p. Bollman (1807), 4 Cr. 75, 94.

[57] In re Savin (1889), 131 U.S. 267. Here the petitioner had been
sentenced to one year in jail for corrupt efforts to intimidate a witness
once in a hallway of the courthouse and once in the jury room, which
were regarded as misbehavior in the presence of the Court. "The
court," declared Justice Harlan, "at least when in session, is present in
every part of the place set apart for its own use, and for the use of its
officers, jurors, and witnesses, and misbehaviour anywhere in such
place is misbehaviour in the presence of the court." 131 U.S. 267, 277;
see also Eilenbecker v. District Court of Plymouth County, *supra*, 36..
"In order that a court may compel obedience to its orders," said Justice Brewer in the Debs case, "it must have the right to inquire whether
there has been any disobedience thereof. To submit the question of
disobedience to another tribunal, be it a jury or another court, would

cerning the power of Congress to require either a trial by jury or trial by another court in criminal contempts.[58] Speaking of the contempt power with reference to jury trial in *Gompers v. Buck's Stove and Range Co.*,[59] Justice Lamar declared:

This power "has been uniformly held to be necessary to the protection of the court from insults and oppressions while in the ordinary exercise of its duties, and to enable it to enforce its judgments and orders necessary to the due administration of law and protection of the rights of suitors."

There has been general recognition of the fact that the courts are clothed with this power and must be authorized to exercise it without referring the issues of fact or law to another tribunal or to a jury in the same tribunal. For if there was no such authority in the first instance there would be no power to enforce its orders if they were disregarded in such independent investigation. Without authority to act promptly and independently the courts could not administer public justice or enforce the rights of private litigants.

None of these expressions, however, was sufficient preparation for the ruling in *Toledo Newspaper Co. v. United States* [60] in 1918, where the Court emasculated the statutory limitations upon the contempt power, ignored the historical background leading to the enactment of the Act of 1831, and overturned past decisions which considered that act as a limitation upon the contempt power.[61] During one of the recurrent contests over

---

operate to deprive the proceeding of half its efficiency." In re Debs (1895), 158 U.S. 564, 595.

[58] In re Debs (1895), 158 U.S. 564; Gompers v. Buck's Stove and Range Co. (1911), 221 U.S. 418; and other cases cited in n. 56.

[59] (1911), 221 U.S. 418, 450.   [60] 247 U.S. 402.

[61] That the Supreme Court had been fully aware of the reasons inducing the limitations imposed by the Act of 1831 is evident in the

rates between a street railway company and its patrons in the city of Toledo, the *News-Bee* had published spirited editorials and lively cartoons on the questions at issue. One of the cartoons depicted the street railway company as a "Moribund man in bed" with one of his friends at the bedside saying, "Guess we'd better call in Doc Killits." Subsequently an injunction was granted by Judge Killits of the United States District Court restraining the enforcement of the low fares provided by ordinance, and other spirited editorials and cartoons followed.

These editorials and cartoons so disturbed the mental equilibrium of Judge Killits that he took up Judge Wilmot's "blaze of glory" and meted out generous punishments to the offenders on the ground that the newspaper articles and cartoons obstructed the administration of justice and constituted attempts to influence and intimidate the mind of the Court. Speaking for himself and four of his brethren, Chief Justice White, who incidentally made the principal contributions to the confusion concerning the power of Congress to define and limit contempts of court, pronounced the Act of 1831 as merely declaratory of the law existing at the time it was passed because Congress had abused its powers to punish for contempt. He cited as his authority the case of *Mar-*

---

opinion of Justice Field in Ex p. Wall (1883), 107 U.S. 265, 302, where he said:

"The power to punish for contempt—a power necessarily incident to all courts for the preservation of order and decorum in their presence—was formerly so often abused for the purpose of gratifying personal dislikes, as to cause general complaint and led to legislation defining the power and designating the cases in which it might be exercised. The act of Congress of March 2, 1831, c. 99, limits the power of courts of the United States."

shall v. Gordon.[62] The language of the Chief Justice is characteristic:

Clarified by the matters expounded and the ruling made in the Marshall Case there can be no doubt that the provision conferred no power not already granted and imposed no limitations not already existing. In other words, it served but to plainly mark the boundaries of the existing authority resulting from and controlled by the grants which the Constitution made and the limitations which it imposed. And this is not at all modified by conceding that the provision was intended to prevent the danger by reminiscence of what had gone before of attempts to exercise a power not possessed which, as pointed out in the Marshall Case, had been sometimes done in the exercise of legislative power.

Stimulated by his success in rendering the statute nugatory, the Chief Justice proceeded to add other fuel to the "blaze of glory" by construing broadly attempts to obstruct the administration of justice or to influence or intimidate the Court. The test to be applied in the former instance is not the actual obstruction resulting from it but rather "the character of the act done and its direct tendency to prevent and obstruct the discharge of judicial duty." Similarly, the criterion of whether a particular act is an attempt to influence or intimidate a court is not the influence exerted upon the mind of a particular judge but "the reasonable tendency of the acts done to influence or bring about the baleful result . . . without reference to the consideration of how far they may have been without influence in a particular case." [63] These tests

----

[62] (1917), 243 U.S. 521, wherein it was held that Congress had no power to punish slanderous and scandalous attacks against it.

[63] Toledo Newspaper Co. v. U.S. (1918), 247 U.S. 402, 418–421. For a criticism of the historical errors committed by the Court in this case,

were applied in *Craig v. Hecht* [64] to sustain the imprisonment of the comptroller of New York City for writing and publishing a letter to a public service commissioner assailing the action of a United States district judge in certain receivership proceedings.

Justice Holmes was correct in his dissent in the *Craig* case when he indicated that unless a judge has power "to lay hold of anyone who ventures to publish anything that tends to make him unpopular or belittle him . . . a man cannot be summarily laid by the heels because his words may make public feeling more unfavorable in case the judge should be asked to act at some later date, any more than he can for exciting feeling against a judge for what he has already done." [65] The plain effect of the *Toledo Newspaper* and *Craig* cases is to transform the inherent power of a court to protect itself against insults and prevent the obstruction of the administration of justice in its presence into the inherent power of a judge to vent his spleen against the particular objects of his personal animosities. The cases convert the natural right of self-preservation existing in courts into a mighty instrument for private vindictiveness. But there is a further effect. The unconscious or deliberate acts of the Court in evading the express terms of a statute by construing such

---

see Frankfurter and Landis, "Power of Congress over Criminal Contempts," 37 Harv. L. Rev. 1010, 1029–1038.

[64] (1923), 263 U.S. 255.

[65] *Ibid.*, 281 ff. "I would go as far as any man," said Justice Holmes, dissenting in the Toledo Newspaper case, "in favor of the sharpest and most summary enforcement of order in court and obedience to decrees, but when there is no need for immediate action contempts are like any other breach of law and should be dealt with as the law deals with other illegal acts. Action like the present, in my opinion, is wholly unwarranted by even color of law." Toledo Newspaper Co. v. U.S. (1918), 247 U.S. 402, 425–426.

terms narrowly when they limit court power and broadly when they confer it tend to create the inference that such statutes would be invalid if they were interpreted to mean what they expressed.

This inference was directly made in 1924 in *Michaelson v. United States* [66] when the Court deliberately placed a restrictive interpretation upon those sections of the Clayton Act relating to contempts in order to avoid serious constitutional questions.

The use of the injunctions by courts to lay down sweeping orders in industrial disputes and then the resort to the powers of contempt to enforce such orders or to punish persons for their disobedience culminated in the inclusion in the Clayton Act [67] of certain provisions designed to prevent what was commonly called "government by injunction." In brief these provisions called for a jury trial upon the demand of the accused in cases of contempt in which the acts committed in violation of an order or process of any district court of the United States or any court of the District of Columbia also constituted a crime under the laws of the United States or those of the state in which they were committed. Section 24 of the act excepted from this provision the summary power of courts to punish "contempt committed in the presence of the court, or so near thereto as to obstruct the administration of justice," and violations of orders entered in suits brought in the name of or on the behalf of the United States.

[66] (1924), 266 U.S. 42.

[67] Act of October 15, 1914, c. 323, secs. 21–25, 38 Stat. at L. 730. For the legislative history of these limitations upon the contempt power, see Frankfurter and Landis, "Power of Congress over Criminal Contempts," 37 Harv. L. Rev. 1038–1042, 1052–1058.

The Circuit Court of Appeals for the Seventh Circuit pronounced these provisions void because they were an unconstitutional attempt of Congress to interrupt the stream of judicial power poured into the vessel of jurisdiction by the Constitution.[68] Thus the inherent power of a court sitting in equity to issue auxiliary writs in aid of its jurisdiction begets the inherent power to punish by summary process the violation of those writs.[69] The Supreme Court of the United States rejected some of the more extravagant assertions of the inferior tribunal and construed strictly the sections in question in order to sustain their validity. Justice Sutherland, speaking for a unanimous court, reaffirmed the authority of Congress to regulate the power to punish contumacious acts by the inferior federal courts but qualified this power by the statement that "the attributes which inhere in that power and are inseparable from it can neither be abrogated nor rendered practically inoperative." Among these inherent attributes Justice Sutherland suggested "the power to deal summarily with contempts committed in the presence of the court or so near thereto as to obstruct the administration of justice" and the power to enforce mandatory decrees by coercive means.[70]

The effect of the cases considered up to this point is that Congress can regulate the inherent power of courts to punish for contempt but that it cannot destroy this power. Congress may require a trial by jury upon the

[68] Michaelson v. U.S. (1923), 291 Fed. 940, 946.

[69] Cf. In re Debs (1895), 158 U.S. 564, 593–596.

[70] Michaelson v. U.S. (1924), 266 U.S. 42, 65–66. The lower federal courts have also narrowly construed the limitations of the Clayton Act. Frankfurter and Landis, "Power of Congress over Criminal Contempts," 1040, n. 110.

demand of the accused in an independent proceeding at law for a criminal contempt which is also a crime, but the power of Congress to provide a jury trial in other criminal contempts is doubtful unless it makes all criminal contempts violations of the laws of the United States. Similarly, the power of Congress to define contempts and limit their scope is doubtful. The development of a theory of constructive contempt in the *Toledo Newspaper* and *Craig* cases renders this power even more doubtful. The phrases "inherent powers" and "in the presence of the court or so near thereto as to obstruct the administration of justice" are a convenient fulcrum by which courts obtain advantageous leverages in any conflict between legislative and judicial authority.

So far, the discussion of the authority of Congress to define and limit contempt of court and prescribe procedure in cases of contempt has related exclusively to the exercise of the contempt power by the courts for the purpose of vindicating their authority and preserving order and decorum in their presence. In the cases dealing with contempt of court a distinction obtains between criminal and civil contempts.[71] Proceedings in criminal contempts are prosecuted for the purpose of vindicating the authority and dignity of the Court and preserving order. Proceedings for civil contempt, on the other hand, are instituted in order to preserve and enforce the rights of the parties to a suit and to compel obedience to orders for the enforcement of rights and preservation of remedies. Punishment in the former proceedings is criminal

[71] Bessette v. W. B. Conkey Co. (1904), 194 U.S. 324, 327–328; Gompers v. Buck's Stove and Range Co. (1911), 221 U.S. 418, 441–443; Ex p. Grossman (1925), 267 U.S. 87.

and punitive; in the latter, coercive and remedial, "and the parties chiefly in interest in their conduct and prosecution are the individuals whose private rights and remedies they were instituted to enforce." [72]

The Court applied this test to contempts in *Ex parte Grossman* [73] and in *Gompers v. Buck's Stove and Range Co.*[74] but modified it to the extent of adding to it the character of the contumacious acts in which a distinction was made between completed and uncompleted contempts of court. A civil contempt results when a person before the Court in a civil case refused to perform an affirmative act in pursuance of a mandatory order. Such a contempt is incomplete and may be purged by performance of the act required in the order or decree of the Court. In criminal contempts, on the other hand, punishment is inflicted for the commission of an act forbidden by the Court. Such an act is a completed contempt, and nothing a defendant can do will purge him of contempt.[75]

Oddly enough, the Court has rarely utilized the distinction between criminal and civil contempts in the cases which involve the authority of Congress to define and limit the contempt power. Since criminal contempts

---

[72] Bessette v. W. B. Conkey Co., 194 U.S. 324, 328; and the cases cited in the preceding notes.

[73] (1925), 267 U.S. 87.   [74] (1911), 221 U.S. 418.

[75] Gompers v. Buck's Stove and Range Co., *supra*, 441–443. The effect of the Gompers and Grossman cases is to make violations of mandatory decrees criminal contempts, and failure to perform a positive act under court order civil contempt. This is not strictly consistent with the other distinction between acts in derogation of court authority and acts required as remedies for private parties. It is quite conceivable that the failure to perform a positive act should be an act solely in derogation of the authority of a court without any relation to the rights of private parties.

are imposed for the purpose of vindicating the authority and dignity of the Court and of preserving order and decorum in its presence, it is logical to infer that criminal contempts would least of all be subject to control or interference by the legislative or executive branches of the government; but this is not true. The President may pardon a criminal contempt,[76] and Congress may require a jury trial in criminal contempts in which the contumacious acts are crimes under the laws of the United States or of the state in which they were committed.[77]

On the other hand, it would seem that, since judicial power is exercised in civil contempts for the protection of the rights of private parties, Congress would have a greater discretion in defining civil contempts. The opposite is true. In the *Grossman* case Chief Justice Taft made it clear that the President cannot pardon a civil or uncompleted contempt,[78] and in the *Michaelson* case Jus-

---

[76] Ex p. Grossman (1925), 267 U.S. 87.

[77] Michaelson v. U.S. (1924), 266 U.S. 42.

[78] Ex p. Grossman, *supra*, 119–120. "A pardon," declared Chief Justice Taft, "can only be granted for a contempt fully completed. Neither in this country nor in England can it interfere with the use of coercive measures to enforce a suitor's right." In answer to the argument that the exercise of the pardoning power in contempt cases violated the principle of the separation of powers and impaired the independence of the judiciary, the Chief Justice replied:

"The Federal Constitution nowhere expressly declares that the three branches of the Government shall be kept separate and independent. All legislative powers are vested in a Congress. The executive power is vested in a President. The judicial power is vested in one Supreme Court and in such inferior courts as Congress may from time to time establish. The judges are given life tenure and a compensation that may not be diminished during their continuance in office, with the evident purpose of securing them and their courts an independence of Congress and the Executive. Complete independence and separation between the branches, however, are not attained, or intended, as other provisions of the Constitution and the normal operation of govern-

tice Sutherland was equally emphatic in denying that
Congress could require a jury trial in cases where the
contemner had failed to perform a mandatory act required for the relief of private parties.[79]

This paradox can be explained partially on the ground
that Congress has always been conceded the widest lati-

---

ment under it easily demonstrate. . . . The fact is that the Judiciary,
quite as much as Congress and the Executive, is dependent on the
cooperation of the other two, that government may go on. Indeed,
while the Constitution has made the Judiciary as independent of the
other branches as is practicable, it is, as often remarked, the weakest
of the three. It must look for a continuity of necessary cooperation,
in the possible reluctance of either of the other branches, to the force
of public opinion."

For diametrically opposed statements with regard to the principle
of the separation of powers, see the opinion of the same chief justice
delivered only one year later in Myers v. U.S. (1926), 272 U.S. 52.

[79] Speaking of the objects regulated by section 22 of the Clayton Act
and the power of the courts to punish for contempt, Justice Sutherland said:

"That the power to punish for contempts is inherent in all courts
has been many times decided and may be regarded as settled law.
It is essential to the administration of justice. The courts of the United
States, when called into existence and vested with jurisdiction over any
subject, at once become possessed of the power. So far as the inferior
federal courts are concerned, however, it is not beyond the authority
of Congress . . . but the attributes which inhere in that power and
are inseparable from it can neither be abrogated nor rendered practically inoperative. That it may be regulated within limits not precisely
defined may not be doubted. The statute now under review is of the
latter character. It is of narrow scope, dealing with the single class
where the act or thing constituting the contempt is also a crime in
the ordinary sense. It does not interfere with the power to deal summarily with contempts committed in the presence of the court or so
near thereto as to obstruct the administration of justice, and in express
terms carefully limited to the cases of contempt specifically defined.
Neither do we think it purports to reach cases of failure or refusal to
comply affirmatively with a decree—that is to do something which a
decree commands—which may be enforced by coercive means or rem-
edied by purely compensatory relief. If the reach of the statute had
extended to the cases which are excluded a different and more serious
question would arise." (1924), 266 U.S. 65–66.

tude in making an act a crime and defining and affixing
the punishment attached to it upon conviction in a court
having jurisdiction of the offense.[80] The presumption of
innocence obtains in criminal contempts as in other criminal actions.[81] Moreover, an act of criminal contempt involves more than interference with the performance of
judicial functions. It is an offense against the governing
authority of the state [82] and may be defined and punished
thereby.

Another explanation that may be advanced is that the
power to punish contempts is solely and strictly a judicial
power which can be exercised only by courts and the
scope of which must be left to judicial determination;
and a second explanation is, therefore, that it has had a
haphazard growth which resulted in seeming contradictions. In the case of *In re Pacific Railway Commission* [83]
Justice Field regarded the contempt power of courts as
so immaculate that it could not be exercised to aid in
compelling witnesses to testify before an investigatory
body created by Congress to investigate the conduct of
railroad companies receiving financial aid from the United
States. In *Interstate Commerce Commission v. Brimson* [84]
Justice Harlan, speaking for the Court, compromised the
virginal purity of the contempt power to the extent of
permitting its use by courts to compel obedience to orders of the Interstate Commerce Commission; but he was

[80] U.S. v. Hudson (1812), 7 Cr. 32; Ex p. Grossman (1925), 267
U.S. 87.
[81] Michaelson v. U.S. (1924), 266 U.S. 42, 66; Gompers v. U.S.
(1914), 233 U.S. 604, 610–611; Gompers v. Buck's Stove and Range Co.
(1911), 221 U.S. 418, 444.
[82] Ex p. Grossman, 267 U.S. 87.   [83] (1887), 32 Fed. 241.
[84] (1894), 154 U.S. 447.

careful to indicate that, except for certain instances in which Congress may exert the authority to punish disorderly behavior, "the power to impose fine or imprisonment in order to compel the performance of a legal duty imposed by the United States, can only be exerted, under the law of the land, by a competent judicial tribunal having jurisdiction in the premises." [85] In his dissent Justice Brewer was certain that "a contempt presupposes some act derogatory to the power and authority of the court," [86] even though he suggested facetiously that the commission might be given the power to punish contempts.

Taken out of the land of its origin where it was first used to vindicate the authority of the King, the power to punish contempts has come to be in the United States a power that is peculiarly and inherently judicial in nature. It is true that in *Anderson v. Dunn* [87] the Court sustained the power of Congress to punish for contempt, but it must be remembered that it confined the exercise of such powers to legislative and judicial bodies. Attorney General Wirt had based his argument on the "natural right of self-defense" and contended that the general grant of judicial power did not preclude other branches of the government from exercising the contempt power which he regarded just as incidental and necessary to a legislature as to a court. The Court rejected the argument of necessity in its extreme form on the ground that

[85] *Ibid.*, 485. As authority for this statement, Justice Harlan cited Whitcomb's Case (1876), 120 Mass. 118, where it was held that the common council of the city of Boston had and could have no power to punish for contempt.

[86] I.C.C. v. Brimson (1894), 154 U.S. 447; 155 U.S. 3, 5.

[87] (1821), 6 Wh. 204.

if it gave such authority to Congress it would likewise confer it upon "every coordinate and even subordinate branch of the government" and lead to "tyrannical licentiousness." [88]

In *Kilbourn v. Thompson* [89] the Court contracted the scope of the *Dunn* case and ruled that Congress had no general power to punish contempts. This holding was based partially upon the ground that Congress was without authority in the original matter but more particularly upon the doctrine of the separation of powers and the strictly judicial nature of the power to impose punishment for contempt. Each of the three departments of the government, according to the Court, is limited by the law of its creation "to exercise of powers appropriate to its own department and no other." The judicial power is vested in one Supreme Court and such inferior courts as Congress may from time to time establish. Hence "no judicial power is vested in the Congress or either branch of it," save in certain exceptional cases. Since a general power to punish for contempt is a strictly judicial power, Congress' power to punish contempt is limited to cases within legitimate legislative cognizance.[90]

Without overruling the rigid restrictions applied to the power of Congress to punish for contempt, the Court has at various times relaxed them to sustain the exercise of congressional power in particular cases. In *McGrain v. Daugherty* [91] the Court sustained the power of the Senate to commit Mally S. Daugherty for contempt because of

[88] *Ibid.*, 228. One of Justice Johnson's reasons for rejecting the argument of necessity was that "the genius and spirit of our institutions are hostile to the exercise of implied powers." P. 225.
[89] (1881), 103 U.S. 168.   [90] *Ibid.*, 190–191, 197.
[91] (1927), 273 U.S. 135.

his refusal to appear, testify, and produce papers upon a subpoena from a Senate committee investigating the Department of Justice. In sustaining the action of the Senate, the Court made it plain that Congress, or either of its branches, "has power through its own process, to compel a private individual to appear before it or one of its committees and give testimony needed to enable it efficiently to exercise a legislative function belonging to it under the Constitution." Although Congress has no general power to conduct inquiries, "the power of inquiry—with process to enforce it—is an essential and appropriate legislative function." Since the investigation in question involved matters upon which Congress might regulate, the action of the Senate was not in excess of congressional power.[92] The assumption of the Court, therefore, seems to be that since Congress needs the contempt power in particular situations, it has it; but it remains for the Court to determine the need for it in a particular case.

The emphasis upon the necessity of Congress' having the power to punish contempts is even greater in *Jurney v. McCracken*[93] where the Court once more distinguished between the facts at hand and the situation in the *Kilbourn* case and sustained the power of the Senate to punish for contempt a witness who destroyed certain papers requested by a Senate committee. The Court rejected McCracken's contention that whatever power Congress had to punish for contempt could be exercised only to remove existing obstructions to legislation and that such power removed or became impossible of removal. Although the Court ruled that no act was punish-

---

[92] *Ibid.,* 154, 161, 173, 174.   [93] (1935), 294 U.S. 125.

able as a contempt of Congress unless it was of a nature to obstruct the performance of legislative duties, it went on to say that the issue presented was "the vindication of the established and essential privilege of requiring the production of evidence." [94]

From *Kilbourn v. Thompson*, where the power to punish for contempt is regarded as so purely judicial that it cannot be sullied by congressional exercise, to *Jurney v. McCracken*, where it is regarded as vested in Congress for the purpose of removing obstacles to legislation and of vindicating congressional authority, is a long step back to *Anderson v. Dunn* and, it would appear, a long step toward a view that administrative agencies have the auxiliary power to remove obstacles to administration and to vindicate their authority. However, the antipathy of the Court to administrative tribunals as expressed in the furiously oracular intonements of Chief Justice Hughes indicates that such a step will not be taken soon. Nevertheless, if the Court regards the power to punish contempts as auxiliary to other powers and a means of vindicating governmental authority, there is no obstacle to its being vested in other governmental agencies as is done in some states.[95] On the other hand, if the contempt power is an essentially judicial power existing in courts per se as agencies independent and distinct from government, other agencies can par-

[94] *Ibid.*, 147–148, 159–160. For a short résumé of Congress' power to punish contempts, see this case further, pp. 148–150. See also In re Chapman (1897), 166 U.S. 661; Marshall v. Gordon (1917), 243 U.S. 521; Harriman v. Interstate Commerce Commission (1908), 211 U.S. 407; Federal Trade Commission v. American Tobacco Co. (1924), 264 U.S. 298; Sinclair v. U.S. (1929), 279 U.S. 263.

[95] See Charles S. Hyneman, "Administrative Adjudication: An Analysis I," 51 Political Science Quarterly 383, 390–392.

ticipate in it only slightly, if at all.[96] More often than not, this has been the attitude of the Supreme Court.

Generally speaking, courts, and courts alone, possess or can possess a general power to punish for contempt. The power exists because it is essential to the preservation of order and decorum in court, to the prevention of obstruction to the administration of justice, and to the enforcement of the orders and decrees of the Court. Regarded as a necessary power incidental to the exercise of jurisdiction, the scope of the contempt power admits of pragmatic tests and of regulation by the legislature in case of abuse. Regarded as an exclusively judicial power which inheres in courts merely because they are courts, it acquires certain psychical qualities that render its precise nature and extent doubtful. In either event the extent of congressional authority as it relates to the power of courts to punish for contempt is finally a matter for judicial determination.

[96] Kilbourn v. Thompson (1881), 103 U.S. 168, 190–191, 197.

CHAPTER IV

LEGISLATIVE COURTS

THUS FAR the discussion relating to courts and the judicial power has dealt exclusively with the Supreme Court and the tribunals constituted inferior to it and with the "judicial power of the United States" vested in such courts by Article III. The power of Congress to establish courts and invest them with judicial power, however, is not exhausted by these provisions of the Constitution. The coefficient clause gives the Congress not only the authority to pass all laws which shall be necessary and proper for the execution of its own powers, but also the power to enact all laws which shall be necessary and proper for executing the powers vested by the Constitution in the general government or in any department or officer thereof.

By virtue of this grant of power, the authority of Congress to create special tribunals and to invest them with special powers and jurisdiction has been recognized by the courts for more than a hundred years.[1] In judicial parlance such courts are commonly designated as legislative courts; but there is no reason why they should not be called administrative or executive courts because, in their essence, they are administrative courts in which are mingled legislative, executive, and judicial functions. Such courts are anomalies in the federal judicial system.

[1] American Insurance Co. v. Canter (1828), 1 Pet. 511, 546.

They are courts but not "courts of the United States." They exercise judicial power but not the "judicial power of the United States." The theoretical limitations of the doctrine of the separation of powers do not apply to them, nor do the prohibitions of Article III, designed for the maintenance of an independent judiciary, protect them.

Almost from the very beginning of the federal system, Congress has exercised its power to create special tribunals and to confer upon them special powers and jurisdiction. As early as 1791, Congress enacted a law authorizing the judges of the circuit courts to settle pension claims against the government subject to legislative and executive revision. Although the judges refused in *Hayburn's Case* [2] to perform this function in their capacity as judges, they did agree to act as commissioners. This was a tacit recognition on the part of the judges that Congress might vest in commissioners jurisdiction over questions susceptible of judicial determination.

In *American Insurance Company v. Canter* [3] the Supreme Court made, for the first time, the distinction between "constitutional" courts and "legislative" courts. This case involved the admiralty jurisdiction of the territorial courts of Florida. Speaking of these courts whose judges were limited to a four-year term in office, Chief Justice Marshall said:

These courts, then, are not constitutional courts, in which the judicial power conferred by the Constitution on the general government can be deposited. They are incapable of receiving it. They are legislative courts created in virtue of the general rights of sovereignty which exists in the government,

[2] (1792), 2 Dall. 409.   [3] (1828), 1 Pet. 511.

or in virtue of that class which enables Congress to make all needful rules and regulations respecting the territory belonging to the United States. The jurisdiction with which they are invested is not a part of that judicial power which that body possesses over the territories of the United States. Although admiralty jurisdiction can be exercised in the States in those courts only which are established in pursuance of the third article of the Constitution, the same limitation does not extend to the territories. In legislating for them, Congress exercises the combined powers of the general and of a State Government.[4]

This distinction between legislative and constitutional courts has been maintained with elaborations ever since. It received its fullest exposition a little more than a century later in *Ex parte Bakelite Corporation* [5] in which the history of legislative courts and the authorities on the power of Congress to create such courts are reviewed at length. The decision in the *Bakelite* case concedes to Congress a wide discretion in establishing administrative tribunals. Other provisions of the Constitution than Article III, it is indicated, delegate to Congress powers in the exercise of which "it may create inferior courts and clothe them with functions deemed essential or helpful in carrying those powers into execution." [6] Such functions are imposed independently of Article III and upon judges who may or may not hold office during good behavior and who may suffer a diminution of salary.

By virtue of its power to "dispose of and make all needful rules and regulations respecting the territory or other property belonging to the United States," Congress' power to establish territorial courts with special

[4] *Ibid.*, 546.   [5] (1929), 279 U.S. 438.
[6] *Ibid.*, 449.

powers and jurisdiction has often been affirmed.[7] Extraterritorial and consular courts have been created for the execution of powers conferred by the Constitution with respect to treaties and foreign commerce.[8] In pursuance of its dual power to constitute tribunals inferior to the Supreme Court and its power of exclusive legislation over the District of Columbia, Congress has created courts for the District. Although these courts are constitutional courts within the meaning of Article III, they possess a dual status and perform dual functions.[9] All of these courts are courts in the real sense of the term and determine matters of private right which in ordinary circumstances could not be withdrawn from the judicial power.

Another class of legislative courts consists of those which are created as special tribunals to determine questions arising between the government and its citizens or

[7] American Insurance Co. v. Canter (1828), 1 Pet. 511, 546; Benner v. Porter (1850), 9 How. 235, 242; Clinton v. Englebrecht (1872), 13 Wall. 434, 447; Good v. Martin (1877), 95 U.S. 90, 98; Reynolds v. U.S. (1878), 98 U.S. 145, 154; The City of Panama (1879), 101 U.S. 453, 460; McAllister v. U.S. (1891), 141 U.S. 174, 180 ff.; Romeu v. Todd (1907), 206 U.S. 358, 368. Cf. O'Donoghue v. U.S. (1933), 289 U.S. 516; Williams v. U.S. (1933), 289 U.S. 553.

[8] U.S. Code, Title 22, secs. 141, 177, 181, 183, 191; In re Ross (1891), 140 U.S. 453; American China Development Co. v. Boyd (C.C., 1906), 148 Fed. 258; Biddle v. U.S. (1907), 84 C.C.A. 415; 156 Fed. 759; Cunningham v. Rodgers (1909), 96 C.C.A. 507; 171 Fed. 835; Swayne & Hoyt v. Everett (1919), 166 C.C.A. 399; 255 Fed. 71; Fleming v. U.S. (C.C.A., 9th Cir., 1922), 279 Fed. 613; Wulfsohn v. Russo-Asiatic Bank (C.C.A., 9th Cir., 1926), 11 F. (2nd) 715.

[9] O'Donoghue v. U.S. (1933), 289 U.S. 516; Postum Cereal Co. v. California Fig Nut Co. (1927), 272 U.S. 693, 700; Keller v. Potomac Electric Power Co. (1923), 261 U.S. 428, 442–444; Butterworth v. U.S. ex rel. Hoe (1884), 112 U.S. 50, 60; U.S. v. Duell (1899), 172 U.S. 576, 582, 583; Federal Radio Commission v. General Electric Co. (1930), 281 U.S. 464, 470.

subjects, which from their nature do not require judicial determination but are susceptible of it. The mode of determining such cases is entirely a matter of legislative discretion. Congress itself might dispose of such questions, or delegate that power to executive departments, or confer it upon judicial tribunals.[10] These matters include claims against the United States,[11] the disposition of the public lands and claims arising therefrom,[12] questions concerning membership in Indian tribes,[13] and questions arising out of the administration of the customs and revenue laws.[14] For the determination of these matters, Congress has provided for a Court of Claims, a Court of Private Land Claims, a Choctaw and Chickasaw Citizenship Court, a Court of Customs Appeals, and a Board of Tax Appeals.[15]

The earliest legislative courts in the United States were the territorial courts created by Congress for the

[10] Ex p. Bakelite Corp. (1929), 279 U.S. 438, 451; Murray v. Hoboken Land and Improvement Co. (1856), 18 How. 272, 280, 284; Grisar v. McDowell (1867), 6 Wall. 363, 379; Auffmordt v. Hedden (1890), 137 U.S. 310, 329; Nishimura Ekiu v. U.S. (1891), 142 U.S. 651, 659, 660; Astiazaran v. Santa Rita Land and Mining Co. (1893), 148 U.S. 80, 81–83; Passavant v. U.S. (1893), 148 U.S. 214, 219; Fong Yue Ting v. U.S. (1893), 149 U.S. 698, 714, 715; U.S. v. Coe (1894), 155 U.S. 76, 84; Wallace v. Adams (1906), 204 U.S. 415, 423; Gordon v. U.S. (1864), 117 U.S. 697, 799; La Abra Silver Mining Co. v. U.S. (1899), 175 U.S. 423, 459–461; U.S. v. Babcock (1919), 250 U.S. 328, 331; Luckenbach Steamship Co. v. U.S. (1926), 272 U.S. 533, 536.

[11] Williams v. U.S. (1933), 289 U.S. 553.

[12] U.S. v. Coe (1894), 155 U.S. 76; Grisar v. McDowell (1867), 6 Wall. 363; Tameling v. U.S. Freehold and Emigration Co. (1876), 93 U.S. 644, 662; Astiazaran v. Santa Rita Land and Mining Co. (1893), 148 U.S. 80, 81–82.

[13] Wallace v. Adams (1907), 204 U.S. 415.

[14] Old Colony Trust Co. v. Commissioner of Internal Revenue (1929), 279 U.S. 716; Ex p. Bakelite Corp. (1929), 279 U.S. 438.

[15] See the cases cited in nn. 11–14.

administration of justice in the territories belonging to the United States. The statutes organizing the government of the territories usually vested the judicial power of the territory in a district court and such other courts as the territorial legislature might establish. The tenure of office of the district judges was usually limited to four years. In numerous instances the district courts of the territories were endowed with the same jurisdiction and powers in cases arising under the Constitution and laws of the United States and cases of admiralty and maritime jurisdiction as the district and circuit courts created under Article III. Such courts, therefore, exercised not only the judicial power of the territory, but applied and administered federal law in the same manner as did constitutional courts.

In spite of the fact that the territorial courts would seem to share in the distribution of the judicial power of the United States mentioned in Article III by virtue of their possessing the same jurisdiction in cases involving a federal question as the ordinary inferior federal courts, such is not the case. Territorial courts have always been held to be legislative as distinguished from constitutional courts and, therefore, incapable of receiving and exercising the judicial power of the United States.[16] Although cases arising under the Constitution and laws of the United States and matters involving private right are a part of the federal judicial power, and

[16] American Insurance Co. v. Canter (1828), 1 Pet. 511, 546; Benner v. Porter (1850), 9 How. 235, 244; Freeborn v. Smith (1865), 2 Wall. 160; Clinton v. Englebrecht (1872), 13 Wall. 434, 449; Hornbuckle v. Toombs (1874), 18 Wall. 648; Good v. Martin (1877), 95 U.S. 90, 98; U.S. v. McMillan (1897), 165 U.S. 504, 510–511; Romeu v. Todd (1907), 206 U.S. 358; Stephens v. Cherokee Nation (1899), 174 U.S. 445.

although no matter which is subject to a suit at the common law, or in equity, or admiralty can be withdrawn from the judicial power and vested in an administrative agency,[17] territorial courts do determine such matters finally subject to appeal to the Supreme Court of the United States.

Since the territorial courts are created under Congress' power to make all needful regulations for the territories of the United States or under an inherent power residing in the sovereignty of the United States, it follows that Congress' power to establish and regulate the jurisdiction and powers of such courts is a plenary power restrained only by those fundamental limitations in the Constitution which are designated for the protection of personal rights. As put by Justice Harlan in the leading case of *McAllister v. United States:*

> The whole subject of the organization of territorial courts, the tenure by which the judges of such courts shall hold their offices, the salary they receive, and the manner in which they may be removed or suspended from office, was left, by the Constitution, with Congress under its plenary power over the territories of the United States.[18]

Accordingly, in enacting legislation affecting the courts of the territories Congress is not limited by the doctrine of the separation of powers.[19] Consequently, legislative, executive, and judicial functions may be merged in prescribing the functions of such courts. Their decisions may be, and have been made, subject to legislative or executive revision even after such decisions or

---

[17] Murray v. Hoboken Land and Improvement Co. (1856), 18 How. 272; Crowell v. Benson (1932), 285 U.S. 22, 50.

[18] (1891), 141 U.S. 174.

[19] Benner v. Porter (1850), 9 How. 235, 242.

decrees have become final.[20] Territorial judges may be removed from office by the President,[21] and their salaries may be reduced during the period for which they were appointed.[22] Finally, in regulating the jurisdiction of territorial courts, Congress may abolish the constitutional distinction between law and equity powers.[23]

Like the territorial courts, the courts of the District of Columbia perform dual functions in administering the laws of the United States and in exercising all the municipal jurisdiction within the District of Columbia. Like the territorial courts, too, they are also dual in status, but their dualism is more pronounced and exists *sui generis* because, unlike territorial courts, the courts of the District of Columbia are constitutional courts and exercise the judicial power of the United States defined in Article III. Although the constitutional law relative to their status and powers is now well settled, there is no uniformity of judicial decision regarding them, and the rulings of the courts are often inconsistent and flatly contradictory. It is necessary, therefore, to trace the chance growth of the courts of the District into constitutional courts through the contradictions of individual decisions.

As early as 1838 in *Kendall v. United States*,[24] the Supreme Court observed that the courts of the District of Columbia were on a different footing from the in-

[20] Wallace v. Adams (1907), 204 U.S. 415; Stephens v. Cherokee Nation (1899), 174 U.S. 445, 471.

[21] McAllister v. U.S. (1891), 141 U.S. 174.

[22] U.S. v. Fisher (1883), 109 U.S. 143.

[23] Hornbuckle v. Toombs (1874), 18 Wall. 648. Cf. Noonan v. Lee, 2 Bl. 499; Orchard v. Hughes, 1 Wall. 73, 77; and Dunphy v. Kleinschmidt, 11 Wall. 610.

[24] 12 Pet. 524.

ferior courts of the United States in that there was no division of powers between the general and municipal government in the District and in that Congress had complete control over the District for every purpose of government.[25] The chief difference, however, was that the Circuit Court for the District was held to be a court of general jurisdiction with the inherent power to issue the writ of mandamus in common-law cases, whereas the inferior courts had previously been held to be courts of special jurisdiction with no inherent power to issue this common-law writ.[26]

Following the distinction made in the *Kendall* case, the Court has frequently sustained the power of Congress to impose nonjudicial functions upon the courts of the District and to limit the finality of their judgments. It has sustained the validity of acts of Congress conferring revisionary powers upon the Supreme Court of the District in patent appeals and making its decisions binding only upon the commissioner of patents.[27] Similarly, the authority of Congress to vest revisionary powers in the Supreme Court of the District over rates fixed by a public utilities commission has been sustained [28] even

[25] *Ibid.*, 619. See also Columbian Insurance Co. v. Wheelright (1822), 7 Wh. 534.

[26] McIntire v. Wood (1813), 7 Cr. 504; McClung v. Silliman (1821), 6 Wh. 598.

[27] Butterworth v. U.S. ex rel. Hoe (1884), 112 U.S. 50; U.S. v. Duell (1899), 172 U.S. 576. Such decisions of the courts of the District, being interlocutory and not final, are not reviewable in the Supreme Court of the United States either by appeal or writ of error. Frasch v. Moore (1908), 211 U.S. 1; E. C. Atkins Co. v. Moore (1909), 212 U.S. 285; Baldwin Co. v. R. S. Howard Co. (1921), 256 U.S. 35. An appeal in such a case was inadvertently permitted in Beckwith v. Commissioner of Patents (1920), 252 U.S. 538. See also Postum Cereal Co. v. California Fig Nut Co. (1927), 272 U.S. 693.

[28] Keller v. Potomac Electric Power Co. (1923), 261 U.S. 428. Here,

though such powers are legislative in nature.[29] The same ruling has been applied to the revisionary power of the Supreme Court of the District over orders of the Federal Radio Commission.[30]

The rulings stated above are all based upon the assumption that the courts of the District of Columbia are legislative courts created by Congress by virtue of its plenary power of government over the District of Columbia. In *Keller v. Potomac Electric Power Co.*[31] the Court ruled that Congress by virtue of its dual authority over the District might vest such jurisdiction and powers in its courts as were exercised in ordinary federal courts and also such as a state might confer upon its courts,[32] but it said nothing concerning the precise status of such courts. In *Federal Radio Commission v. General Electric Co.*,[33] involving a similar state of facts, the Court reached the same conclusion on the ground that such courts were legislative courts. Likewise, in *Ex parte Bakelite Corporation*[34] the Court said by way of obiter that the courts of the District were legislative and not constitutional courts.[35] In the *Federal Radio Commission* case an appeal

too, it was held that an appeal would not lie to the Supreme Court of the United States because the action of the lower court was legislative and not judicial.

[29] Prentis v. Atlantic Coast Line R. Co. (1908), 211 U.S. 210; Keller v. Potomac Electric Power Co. (1923), 261 U.S. 428.

[30] Federal Radio Commission v. General Electric Co. (1930), 281 U.S. 464.

[31] (1923), 261 U.S. 428.

[32] *Ibid.*, 442–443. Citing Kendall v. U.S. (1838), 12 Pet. 524, 619; Butterworth v. U.S. ex rel. Hoe (1884), 112 U.S. 50, 60; U.S. v. Duell (1899), 172 U.S. 576; Baldwin Co. v. R. S. Howard Co. (1921), 256 U.S. 35.

[33] (1930), 281 U.S. 464.   [34] (1929), 279 U.S. 438.

[35] *Ibid.*, 450. Citing Keller v. Potomac Electric Power Co. (1923), 261 U.S. 428, 442 ff.; Postum Cereal Co. v. California Fig Nut Co.

had been taken from the refusal of the commission to renew a license to the Court of Appeals of the District of Columbia. Section 16 of the Radio Commission Act provided for appeals from the commission to the Court of Appeals and authorized that court to "hear, review, and determine the appeal" upon the record and evidence of the commission and such additional evidence as the Court might receive. The Court of Appeals was further authorized to alter or revise the decision of the commission and to enter such judgment as the Court might think just. These provisions for appeal were held to do nothing more than make the Court "a superior and revising agency in the same field." [36] To justify this merging of administrative and judicial functions, the Court cited the *Keller, Butterworth,* and *Postum Cereal Company* cases and said of them with reference to the courts of the District of Columbia:

In the cases just cited, as also in others, it is recognized that courts of the District of Columbia are not created under the judiciary article of the Constitution, but are legislative courts, and therefore that Congress may vest them with jurisdiction and powers, such as have been just described.[37]

These decisions are in accord with those relating to the territorial courts and are consistent within themselves. They all recognize that the courts of the District of Columbia are created under Congress' plenary power of legislation over the District and hold by implication

---

(1927), 272 U.S. 693, 700; Butterworth v. U.S. ex rel. Hoe (1884), 112 U.S. 50, 60; U.S. v. Duell (1899), 172 U.S. 576, 582–583.

[36] 281 U.S. 464, 467.

[37] *Ibid.,* 468. The Court itself refused to hear the case on a writ of certiorari for lack of jurisdiction to entertain appeals from mere administrative decisions. P. 469.

that the third article of the Constitution does not apply to the District of Columbia. Although the Supreme Court had previously ruled that the Supreme Court of the District was a court of the United States within the meaning of section 714 of the revised statutes, the question of whether it was a constitutional court of the United States was left undecided.[38] A preponderance of judicial precedent, therefore, led to the professional belief that they were legislative courts and that the judicial article did not apply to the District of Columbia.[39]

In 1933 the holding of the *Federal Radio Commission* case and the dictum in the *Bakelite* case were reversed by the ruling in *O'Donoghue v. United States* [40] that the courts of the District of Columbia were constitutional courts. Because of the reversal of earlier precedents and the attempt of the Court to reconcile its ruling with prior decisions, the *O'Donoghue* case deserves special consideration.

Under the appropriations act of 1932 which reduced the salaries of all judges except those whose compensation might not be diminished under the Constitution, the Comptroller General decided that the courts of the District of Columbia were legislative courts the judges of which were not protected by Article III, section 1, of the Constitution. Averring patriotic rather than mere personal economic interests in this ruling, a judge of the Supreme Court of the District and a judge of the Court of Appeals brought suit in the Court of Claims to recover

[38] James v. U.S. (1906), 202 U.S. 401.
[39] See Katz, "Federal Legislative Courts" (1930), 43 Harv. L. Rev. 894–924, wherein the courts of the District of Columbia are treated as legislative courts.
[40] 289 U.S. 516.

the amount of the deductions. The Court of Claims did not determine the case but certified the constitutional questions to the Supreme Court for its determination.

Starting with the proposition that the separation of powers is basic and vital to the American system, the Court found that the reasons impelling the adoption of the prohibition against the diminution of judicial salaries [41] applied with even greater force to the courts of the District than to other federal courts "because the judges of the former courts are in closer contact with, and more immediately open to the influences of, the legislative department, and exercise a more extensive jurisdiction in cases affecting the operations of the general government and its various departments." [42] Having already reached the conclusion that there was nothing "in the Constitution, or in the character or organization of the District, or its relation to the general government, or in the character of the courts themselves," which precluded their being equal in rank and power with the other inferior federal courts, the Court merely had to justify its position.

The first step in the reasoning of the Court is its distinction between the transitory nature of the territories and their government [43] on the one hand and the permanency of the District of Columbia and its governmental organization on the other. The territories are in a state of temporary pupilage, and, in establishing ter-

[41] For these reasons see Evans v. Gore (1920), 253 U.S. 245.

[42] 289 U.S. 516, 535.

[43] For the temporary character of territorial organization and government, see McAllister v. U.S. (1891), 141 U.S. 174; Downes v. Bidwell (1901), 182 U.S. 244, 293 (concurring opinion of White, J.); Snow v. U.S. (1874), 18 Wall. 317; Pollard v. Hagan (1845), 3 How. 212, 224.

ritorial courts, Congress is acting independently of the Constitution upon territory which is not a part of the United States and to which the third article of the Constitution has no application.[44] "How different are the status and characteristics of the District of Columbia!" exclaimed Justice Sutherland. "The District, as the seat of the national government, is as lasting as the states from which it was carved or the union whose permanent capital it became." [45] Accordingly, the District of Columbia is a part of the United States upon which the judicial power of the United States, as defined in Article III, operates, and its courts are constitutional courts exercising the judicial power of the United States. They are permanent establishments and form a permanent part of the federal judicial system. In the sphere of federal jurisdiction their parallelism with the other inferior courts is complete.[46] Accordingly, the judges of such courts are protected by the provisions for tenure during good behavior and by the prohibition against any diminution of salary during their continuance in office. Congress can neither limit their tenure nor diminish their salaries although it possesses plenary governmental power over the District by virtue of Article I, section 8, clause 17.

If such courts are constitutional courts, how is it that

[44] 289 U.S. 516, 542, citing and quoting with approval the opinion of Brown, J., in Downes v. Bidwell (1901), 182 U.S. 244, 266.

[45] 289 U.S. 516, 538.

[46] Ibid., 540–544. Cf. Federal Trade Commission v. Klesner (1927), 274 U.S. 145, 154; Claiborne-Annapolis Ferry Co. v. U.S. (1932), 285 U.S. 382, 390. If the District of Columbia courts are constitutional courts because the judicial article applies to the District as a part of the United States, it would seem to follow that the judicial power of the United States operates upon the incorporated territories of the United States and that their courts are likewise constitutional courts.

Congress can constitutionally impose nonjudicial functions upon them? The answer to this question constitutes
the second step in Justice Sutherland's argument wherein
he undertakes to reconcile the ruling at hand with previous decisions. In establishing courts for the District of
Columbia, Congress is performing a dual function and
acting under two distinct powers. It is exercising its power
to establish tribunals inferior to the Supreme Court of
the United States and also its plenary and exclusive power
of legislation over the District. Article III, section 1, limits
this plenary power of legislation in so far as the tenure
and salaries of the judges are concerned but not with regard to the conferring of legislative and administrative
functions of the Court.[47]

"The fact," says the Court, "that Congress, under another and plenary grant of power has conferred upon
these courts jurisdiction over non-federal causes of action, or over quasi-judicial or administrative matters does
not affect the question. In dealing with the District, Congress possesses the powers which belong to it in respect
of territory within a state, and also the powers of a
state." [48] Thus the dual powers of Congress over the District enable it to confer dual powers upon its courts and
to endow them with a dual status. Subject to the guarantees of personal liberty in the Constitution, "Congress has
as much power to vest courts of the District with a variety
of jurisdiction and powers as a state legislature has in conferring jurisdiction on its courts." [49] But how, one is

[47] 289 U.S. 516, 545, 546.   [48] *Ibid.*, 545.
[49] *Ibid.*, citing Prentis v. Atlantic Coast Line R. Co. (1908), 211 U.S.
210, 225, to the effect that a state legislature may unite legislative and
judicial functions in the courts of a state.

From these views of the majority, Chief Justice Hughes and Justices

entitled to ask, are such contradictions to be reconciled? The two functions are not incompatible, says the Court; but this is not sufficient. The only answer is that in creating such courts Congress derives its power from Article III and must act within the limits of that article, and that, in conferring jurisdiction and powers upon such courts, Congress is acting in pursuance of its plenary power to legislate for the District independently of Article III and therefore free from its limitations.

Like the status of the courts of the District of Columbia, that of the Court of Claims has not always been certain. In the earliest cases involving the Court of Claims it was regarded as a legislative court, but in subsequent decisions it came to be regarded in dicta as a constitutional court.[50] A preponderance of judicial opinion, however, fixes the character of the Court of Claims as a legislative court created by Congress to perform special functions.[51]

Until 1855 either Congress or the executive depart-

Van Devanter and Cardozo dissented on the ground that the plenary power of Congress over the District of Columbia is complete in itself and derives nothing from the judicial article. In other words, Congress' power over the District is the same as its power over the territories. The dissenting judges regarded the power of Congress over the District not as a dual power in the sense that it is derived from the first and third articles but only in the sense that the first article confers authority so broad that it enables Congress to invest courts of the District not only with jurisdiction and powers analogous to those of United States courts, but also with jurisdiction and powers analogous to those of state courts. 289 U.S. 516, 552.

[50] U.S. v. Klein (1872), 13 Wall. 128, 145; U.S. v. Union Pacific R. Co. (1879), 98 U.S. 569, 603; Minnesota v. Hitchcock (1902), 185 U.S. 373, 386; Kansas v. U.S. (1907), 204 U.S. 331, 342; U.S. v. Louisiana (1887), 123 U.S. 32, 35. See also Miles v. Graham (1925), 268 U.S. 501.

[51] Gordon v. U.S. (1864), 117 U.S. app. 697; In re Sanborn (1893), 148 U.S. 222; U.S. v. Babcock (1919), 250 U.S. 328; McElrath v. U.S. (1880), 102 U.S. 426; Ex p. Bakelite Corp. (1929), 279 U.S. 438, 451–455; Williams v. U.S. (1933), 289 U.S. 553.

ments determined all claims arising against the government of the United States: In that year Congress created the Court of Claims and empowered it to examine and determine all claims against the government within certain classes.[52] In the beginning the decisions of the Court were merely advisory and were subject to executive and legislative revision. After the refusal of the Supreme Court to hear an appeal from the judgment of the Court of Claims, Congress has from time to time modified the original act by making some of its judgments binding and by extending its jurisdiction,[53] and today the Court of Claims continues to render both final judgments and advisory opinions.[54] It is, therefore, both a judicial and investigatory body.

Congress' power to create the Court of Claims is derived from two sources. In the first place, Congress is empowered by the eighth section of the first article of the Constitution to pay the debts of the United States, and, in so doing, it has the incidental power to determine what claims shall be paid. Congress may determine these claims itself; or it may delegate this power to the executive departments, to the courts of law, or to special tribunals. Second, the United States cannot be sued without its consent. As the legislative branch of the government, Congress has the authority to determine when and under

[52] Act of Feb. 24, 1855, c. 122, 10 Stat. at L. 612.
[53] Act of Mar. 3, 1863, c. 92, secs. 3, 5, and 7, 12 Stat. at L. 765; Act of Mar. 17, 1866, c. 19, 14 Stat. at L. 9; Act of Mar. 3, 1883, c. 116, secs. 1, 2, 22 Stat. at L. 485; Act of Jan. 20, 1885, c. 25, sec. 6, 23 Stat. at L. 283; Act of Mar. 3, 1887, c. 359, secs. 12–14, 24 Stat. at L. 505.
[54] For the present jurisdiction of the Court of Claims, see U.S. Code, Title 28, secs. 250, 251, 259, 268.

what conditions the government may be sued.[55] Such conditions may be arbitrary and even obnoxious, but a suitor implicitly consents to them when he brings suit against the government. This follows from the general rule that when the United States creates rights in individuals against itself, it is under no obligation to provide a remedy through the courts for the protection of such rights,[56] and from the related rule that where a statute creates a right and provides a special remedy, that remedy is exclusive.[57]

This authority of Congress over the Court of Claims has long been recognized. Chief Justice Taney in his last judicial utterance in the *Gordon* case [58] conceded the undoubted authority to establish "tribunals with special powers to examine testimony and decide, in the first instance, upon the validity and justice of any claim for

[55] U.S. v. Babcock (1919), 250 U.S. 328; McElrath v. U.S. (1880), 102 U.S. 426.

[56] U.S. v. Babcock, *supra;* U.S. v. Black (1888), 128 U.S. 40; Ex p. Atocha (1874), 17 Wall. 439; Gordon v. U.S. (1869), 7 Wall. 188, 195; De Groot v. U.S. (1867), 5 Wall. 419, 431–433; Comegys v. Vasse (1828), 1 Pet. 193, 212.

[57] Wilder Mfg. Co. v. Corn Products Co. (1915), 236 U.S. 165, 175; Arnson v. Murphy (1883), 109 U.S. 238; Barnet v. Muncie Nat. Bank (1879), 98 U.S. 555, 558; Farmers' & Mechanics' National Bank v. Dearing (1876), 91 U.S. 29, 35. The leading case in which these rules were applied to the Court of Claims is U.S. v. Babcock (1919), 250 U.S. 328, 331, where the Court of Claims was held without jurisdiction to review the determination of the Auditor of the War Department under a statute providing for the recovery of compensation by men enlisted in the military or naval service for loss of privately owned personal property. See also McElrath v. U.S. (1880), 102 U.S. 426, where it was held that Congress could constitutionally give the Court of Claims jurisdiction to render a final judgment, subject to appeal in favor of the United States for setoffs and counterclaims without providing for a jury trial.

[58] Gordon v. U.S. (1864), 117 U.S. app. 697.

money against the United States, subject to the supervision and control of Congress, or a head of any of the executive departments." [59] That Taney did not regard the Court of Claims and other legislative courts as courts in the real sense of the term is clear from his opinions in the *Gordon* case and in *United States v. Ferreira*.[60] The circumstances that the Court of Claims was called a court and its decisions called judgments could neither, in Taney's view, "alter its character nor enlarge its power." Legislative courts, in his opinion, were mere commissions exercising judicial power in the sense that they were required to use judgment and discretion. Such power, however, was not judicial in the sense in which the judicial power was granted by the Constitution to the courts of the United States.[61]

The Court of Claims, being a legislative court, therefore depends for its existence and all of its powers upon congressional enactment. The limitations of the separation of powers do not apply to it, and the provisions of

[59] *Ibid.*, 699.   [60] (1852), 13 How. 40.
[61] Referring to the powers conferred upon the United States district judge for the District of Florida to examine claims arising under the Spanish treaty and report his decisions and the evidence upon which they were founded to the Secretary of the Treasury, the Chief Justice said: "The powers conferred by these acts of Congress upon the judge as well as the Secretary, are, it is true, judicial in their nature. For judgment and discretion must be exercised by both of them. But it is nothing more than the power ordinarily given by law to a commissioner appointed to adjust claims to lands or money under a treaty; or special powers to inquire into or decide any other particular class of controversies in which the public or individuals may be concerned. A power of this description may constitutionally be conferred on a secretary as well as on a commission. But it is not judicial in either case, in the sense in which judicial power is granted by the Constitution to the courts of the United States." U.S. v. Ferreira (1852), 13 How. 40, 48.

Article III do not protect the compensation and tenure of its judges.[62] It exercises and can exercise no part of the judicial power of the United States.[63]

Like the Court of Claims, the Court of Customs and Patent Appeals is a legislative court and is subject to the same general rules that apply to the Court of Claims with relation to legislative authority over the powers, jurisdiction, and process of the Court itself and the tenure and salary of its judges. The question of the status of this court, as the former Court of Customs Appeals prior to 1929, arose in 1929 in *Ex parte Bakelite Corporation.*[64] The petitioner had sought a writ of prohibition against an appeal from the tariff commission to the Court of Customs Appeals on the ground that the tribunal was a constitutional court and could have no jurisdiction over any proceeding which was not a case or controversy, and that the proceeding before the commission was not a case or controversy but merely an advisory opinion in aid of executive action. The Court rejected these conten-

---

[62] Williams v. U.S. (1933), 289 U.S. 553, 581. See, however, Miles v. Graham (1925), 268 U.S. 501, where it was held on the authority of Evans v. Gore (1920), 253 U.S. 245, that Congress could not include the salary of a judge of the Court of Claims in income upon which he was required to pay a tax. For purposes of salary the Court of Claims was regarded as a court of the United States within the meaning of the third article.

[63] Williams v. U.S., *supra*, 579. Justice Sutherland's refusal to follow the dictum in the Bakelite case concerning the status of the courts of the District of Columbia in O'Donoghue v. U.S. and his eagerness to accept the dictum in the same case concerning the Court of Claims is interesting. The statements in the Bakelite case concerning the courts of the District were dismissed as obiter dicta. In Williams v. U.S. the dicta in the Bakelite case relating to the Court of Claims were treated as being fortified by reasoning and illustration and as "the result of a careful review of the entire matter." 289 U.S. 553, 571.

[64] 279 U.S. 438.

tions and ruled that the Court was a legislative tribunal charged with administrative functions.[65]

What, it may be asked, is it that determines whether a tribunal is a constitutional or legislative court? The distinction is a tenuous one and depends for its existence not upon the tenure by which the judges of a court hold office, or upon the organization of the Court, or yet upon the will or intention of Congress. The true test of the

[65] This ruling was consistent with the legislative history of the Court of Customs Appeals and the Court of Customs. The Payne-Aldrich tariff bill of 1909 contained a provision for a court of customs appeals with jurisdiction to determine finally appeals from the board of general appraisers. The purpose of the provision was to facilitate a more efficient administration of the customs laws and to relieve the Supreme Court from the excessive burdens of customs litigation. The proposal was supported in the Senate by Aldrich, Lodge, and other "Old Guard" Republicans, and was opposed by Borah, Cummins, Clapp, Dolliver, and other insurgents who regarded the creation of such a court as an attempt of the government to create a special tribunal in which its viewpoint would be favorably received and, therefore, as an indefensible impeachment of the judicial systems. Speech of Senator Borah, July 7, 1909, 44 Cong. Rec. 4191. Senator Cummins disliked the provisions for finality. Senators Bailey and McCumber answer these criticisms by asserting that the purpose of the Court was not to give advantage to the government over the importer but to remove the advantage of the importer over the government in the administration of the customs. Senator Flint pointed to the congested dockets of the federal courts and averred that the purpose of the Court was to remove this congestion and provide for a uniform interpretation of the customs laws by highly trained and specialized customs authorities. 44 Cong. Rec. 4191–4225. The insurgents took the same position on the bill to create the Commerce Court. See Frankfurter and Landis, *The Business of the Supreme Court* (New York, 1928), 153–174, for the legislative history of the ill-fated Commerce Court.

For the provisions governing the Court of Customs Appeals, see Act of August 5, 1909, c. 6, sec. 29, 36 Stat. at L. 105; Judicial Code, secs. 188–199. In 1926 Congress changed the name of the board of general appraisers to the Court of Customs without altering its nature, powers, functions, or personnel. Act of May 28, 1926, c. 411, 44 Stat. at L. 669.

status of a court "lies in the power under which the court was created and in the jurisdiction conferred." [66] Accordingly, whether a tribunal is a legislative or constitutional court is finally a question for judicial determination.

Not the least important aspect of a federal system of administrative tribunals is the appellate jurisdiction of the Supreme Court of the United States over their judgments and decrees. The Supreme Court, as has been demonstrated in an earlier chapter, can perform only judicial functions. It can review only judicial judgments in a real case or controversy, and it can exercise no revisory power over the decrees of an administrative agency. Lastly, its decrees must be final, and they cannot be subjected to administrative or legislative revision.[67] It is clear, then, that the Supreme Court cannot review the interlocutory decrees or administrative findings of legislative courts.[68]

This received great emphasis in Chief Justice Taney's last judicial opinion, but Taney went much further than this. In his view the Supreme Court could never review the judgments and decrees of legislative courts. As put by the great chief justice with reference to the appellate jurisdiction of the Supreme Court and legislative courts:

The appellate power and jurisdiction are subject to such exceptions and regulations as the Congress shall make. But the appeal is given only from such inferior courts as Congress may ordain and establish to carry into effect the judicial

---

[66] Ex p. Bakelite Corp. (1929), 279 U.S. 438, 459.   [67] Chap. 1.

[68] Gordon v. U.S. (1864), 117 U.S. app. 697; U.S. v. Ferreira (1852), 13 How. 40; In re Sanborn (1893), 148 U.S. 222; Frasch v. Moore (1908), 211 U.S. 1; E. C. Atkins Co. v. Moore (1909), 212 U.S. 285; Baldwin Co. v. R. S. Howard Co. (1921), 256 U.S. 35; Postum Cereal Co. v. California Fig Nut Co. (1927), 272 U.S. 693; Keller v. Potomac Electric Power Co. (1923), 261 U.S. 428; Federal Radio Commission v. General Electric Co. (1930), 281 U.S. 464.

204 JUDICIAL POWER OF THE UNITED STATES

power specifically granted to the United States. The inferior
court, therefore, from which the appeal is taken, must be a
judicial tribunal authorized to render a judgment which will
bind the rights of the parties litigating before it, unless ap-
pealed from, and upon which the appropriate process of execution may be issued by the Court to carry it into effect. . . .
And it is very clear that this Court has no appellate power
over these special tribunals, and cannot, under the Constitution, take jurisdiction of any decision, upon appeal, unless it
was made by an inferior court, exercising independently the
judicial power granted to the United States.[69]

These views were tacitly rejected three years later in
De Groot v. United States [70] when the Supreme Court
took an appeal from a final judgment of the Court of
Claims without questioning its jurisdiction. Since then the
authority of the Court to exercise appellate jurisdiction
has depended, not upon the nature or status of the Court
from which the appeal comes, but upon the nature of the
proceeding before the lower court and the finality of its
judgment. Accordingly, in proceedings before a legislative court which are judicial in their nature and admit of
a final judgment, subject only to appeal, the Supreme
Court may be vested with appellate jurisdiction, even
though legislative courts exercise no part of the judicial
power of the United States, and in spite of the rule that
the Supreme Court may exercise no other power.[71]

However, before the Court can review the proceedings

[69] Gordon v. U.S. (1864), 117 U.S. app. 697, 702 ff.
[70] (1867), 5 Wall. 419.
[71] The same anomaly exists in the power of the Supreme Court to
review the judgments and decrees of state courts in cases involving
a federal question and in the absolute lack of power of state courts
to share in the exercise of the judicial power of the United States. On
this point see Cohens v. Virginia (1821), 6 Wh. 264; Martin v. Hunter's
Lessee (1816), 1 Wh. 304; Teal v. Felton, 12 How. 284.

of a legislative court, the proceedings must be judicial in nature, and the judgments or decrees rendered therein must be final and conclusive. In other words, the issues involved must be duly presented in an actual case or controversy. The Supreme Court will not review the legislative or administrative proceedings of administrative tribunals or the courts of the District of Columbia,[72] and it will not entertain appeals from the advisory or interlocutory opinions or decrees of such tribunals.[73]

The operation of this rule is well illustrated in *Keller v. Potomac Electric Power Co.*,[74] *Federal Radio Commission v. General Electric Co.*,[75] and *Federal Radio Commission v. Nelson Brothers Bond and Mortgage Co.*[76] The *Keller* case involved the validity of a provision of the public utilities law of the District of Columbia which gave the utility commission the right by action in equity to seek the advice of the Supreme Court of the District upon the elements of value to be considered in arriving at a true valuation for rate-making purposes, and which further granted the right to any person or utility to institute a proceeding in equity in the Supreme Court to vacate, set aside, or modify any order of the commission on the ground of inadequacy or unreasonableness. The Supreme Court of the United States ruled that the functions of the Court of the District were legislative in nature and held, therefore, that the provision in question was invalid in

---

[72] Keller v. Potomac Electric Power Co. (1923), 261 U.S. 428; Federal Radio Commission v. General Electric Co. (1930), 281 U.S. 464; cf. Prentis v. Atlantic Coast Line R. Co. (1908), 211 U.S. 210.

[73] Postum Cereal Co. v. California Fig Nut Co. (1927), 272 U.S. 693; Butterworth v. U.S. ex rel. Hoe, 112 U.S. 50.

[74] (1923), 261 U.S. 428. [75] (1930), 281 U.S. 464.

[76] (1933), 289 U.S. 266.

so far as it granted the right of appeal from the lower tribunal to the Supreme Court.

The first *Radio Commission* case came to the Court on a writ of certiorari from the Court of Appeals of the District of Columbia. The Radio Commission Act provided for appeals from the commission to the Court of Appeals and authorized the latter to take additional evidence that it deemed proper, to hear and determine the appeal upon such record and evidence, and to alter or revise the decision of the commission and render such judgment that it deemed just. On the ground that this provision did nothing more than make the Court of Appeals "a superior and revising agency in the same field," the Supreme Court refused to entertain the case on certiorari.

This provision of the federal radio act was amended in 1930 so as to limit the jurisdiction of the Court of Appeals in such cases to matters of law in which its decisions were made final subject to appeal. In the second *Radio Commission* case the Court held that it could entertain an appeal in such cases in view of the statutory amendment.[77]

In the preceding pages the power of Congress to create special tribunals for the final determination of administrative questions has been demonstrated to admit of no doubt. But how far does this power extend? To what extent may Congress vest the final disposition of questions judicial in nature in special courts that exercise and can

[77] For the original provision see the Federal Radio Act of Feb. 23, 1927, c. 69, sec. 16, 44 Stat. at L. 1169. For the amendment see Act of July 1, 1930, c. 788, 46 Stat. at L. 844. For another case similar to the Keller and Federal Radio Commission cases, see Postum Cereal Co. v. California Fig Nut Co. (1927), 272 U.S. 693, 698–699.

exercise no part of the judicial power of the United States? Finally, what are the possibilities of a separate system of administrative courts and administrative law in the United States, and is there a possibility that in the branches of government, at least, the *droit administratif* will supersede the late Professor Dicey's cherished "rule of law"?

The answers to these questions involve not only such intricate constitutional questions as the finality of administrative action in the light of the due process clause of the Fifth Amendment, but also important aspects of practical political science, of government, and of administration. As the functions of government become more complex and diffused by the continuous extension of governmental authority over private and collective action, new problems of administration always arise, and sometimes old ones become more acute. The application of new principles of governmental control and regulation or the extension of old principles always demands either the creation of new administrative machinery or an improvement in the old methods of administration.

That courts of justice cannot adequately perform the new functions of government which have arisen out of an advanced sense of social responsibility and the increasing necessity of social control is apparent. The nature of the judicial process, the technique of the judges, and the inflexibility of judicial forms are all unadaptable to the administration of laws which require summary action for their efficient execution. The administration of justice in the courts requires a certain slowness of deliberation; the administration of laws relating to health, public utilities, taxation, industrial relations, and so on requires hasty action unhampered by litigation in the courts. Litigation, if it must come, must follow administrative action.

The attitude of the Supreme Court of the United States toward the new reform in judicial procedure known as the declaratory judgment is sufficient evidence that the old forms of procedure and the old methods of technique that unfit courts for the effective administration of the social functions of government are likely to remain for a long time and that any radical reform in judicial procedure is far removed if not impossible. Moreover, such a change in the organization and procedure in courts of justice that would enable them efficiently to administer the duties thrust upon government by an industrial society would incapacitate them in the execution of their normal and accustomed powers. A new method must be devised.

The intelligent application of laws relating to patents, the customs, interstate commerce, industrial relations, economic planning, and the like requires more than a knowledge of the law. It requires the application of a mechanical and scientific technique and of a highly specialized knowledge. It also requires a tolerance for new forms of state activity. Many courts must, therefore, be special courts manned with experts, endowed with new forms of procedure, and vested with the power to render decisions to which is attached all the sanctity of judicial finality.

There are three solutions to this problem, all of which tend to remove the disadvantages of the government as a litigant seeking to administer its laws in the ordinary courts and at the same time to provide ample protection for the rights of the individual. One solution is the establishment of specialized courts for the administration of particular laws and investing them with the judicial power of the United States as was done in the creation of the ill-fated Commerce Court.[78] Second, Congress may establish legislative courts, vest them with administrative or legislative powers, and provide no means of appeal as was done in the statutes involved in the *Keller* and *Radio Commission* cases, or it may vest them with judicial functions from which an appeal to courts of the United States may be taken. Finally, Congress may make the decisions of legislative courts final and withdraw the right of appeal to regularly constituted judicial tribunals exercising the judicial power of the United States.

It is the last of these possibilities that raises the most serious constitutional questions both with regard to the creation of legislative courts and the vesting of judicial finality in them. In the first place, although Congress derives no power to create legislative courts from Article III, this power is in fact limited by the judicial article. This is true because Congress can neither "withdraw from judicial cognizance any matter which, from its nature, is the subject of a suit at the common law, or in equity, or admiralty; nor, on the other hand, can it bring under the judicial power a matter which, from its nature, is not a subject for judicial determination. At the same time there

[78] For the history of the Commerce Court, its creation, and abolition, see Frankfurter and Landis, *The Business of the Supreme Court* (New York, 1928), 153-174. On the general subject of legislative courts or administrative tribunals, see especially the following articles: Katz, "Federal Legislative Courts" (1930), 43 Harv. L. Rev. 894; Pillsbury, "Administrative Tribunals" (1923), 36 Harv. L. Rev. 405; Lilienthal, "The Power of Governmental Agencies to Compel Testimony" (1926), 39 Harv. L. Rev. 694; Biklé, "Judicial Determination of Questions of Fact Affecting the Constitutional Validity of Legislative Action" (1925), 38 Harv. L. Rev. 6; and the articles of Professor Powell in (1913), 28 Political Science Quarterly 34, (1907), 1 American Pol. Sci. Rev. 583, and (1911), 24 Harv. L. Rev. 333, 441.

are matters, involving public rights, which may be presented in such form that the judicial power is capable of acting on them, and which are susceptible of judicial determination, but which Congress may or may not bring within the cognizance of the courts of the United States, as it may deem proper." [79]

This rule, first enunciated in 1856, was elaborated and explained three-quarters of a century later in *Crowell v. Benson*,[80] in which the Court made a distinction between cases of private right and cases arising between the government and persons subject to its authority in connection with the performance of the constitutional function of the legislative and executive departments. Referring to the question of whether the Longshoremen's and Harbor Workers' Compensation Act vested power finally to determine matters of fact upon which depended questions of law in an executive officer, the Court said:

In relation to these basic facts, the question is not the ordinary one as to the propriety of provision for administrative determinations. Nor have we simply the question of due process in relation to notice and hearing. It is rather a question of the appropriate maintenance of the Federal judicial power in requiring the observance of constitutional restrictions. It is the question whether the Congress may substitute for constitutional courts, in which the judicial power of the

[79] Murray v. Hoboken Land and Improvement Co. (1856), 18 How. 272, 284; Crowell v. Benson (1932), 285 U.S. 22, 50.

[80] *Supra*. This distinction was made in the Murray case, but it was not stressed. Indeed, the Court recognized that executive determinations of matters of private right might, under certain conditions, be conclusive. Said the Court: "It is true, also, that even in a suit between private persons to try a question of private right, the action of the executive power, upon a matter committed to its determination by the Constitution and laws, is conclusive." (1856), 18 How. 272, 284, 285.

United States is vested, an administrative agency—in this instance a single deputy commissioner—for the final determination of the existence of the facts upon which the enforcement of the constitutional rights of the citizen depend. The recognition of the utility and convenience of administrative agencies for the investigation and finding of facts within their proper province . . . does not require the conclusion that there is no limitation of their use, and that the Congress could completely oust the courts of all determinations of fact by vesting the authority to make them with finality in its own instrumentalities or in the Executive Department. That would be to sap the judicial power as it exists under the Federal Constitution, and to establish a government of a bureaucratic character alien to our system, wherever fundamental rights depend, as not infrequently they do depend, upon the facts, and finality as to facts becomes in effect finality in law.[81]

The action of the Court in sustaining the lower tribunal in permitting a trial *de novo* of the facts and the strong language used by the Court with reference to the lack of authority in Congress to oust the federal courts from the exercise of federal judicial power and substitute therefor its own instrumentalities justify the conclusion that the *Crowell* case throws definite limitations upon the power of Congress to establish legislative courts which, in the last analysis, are, in the light of judicial precedent, instrumentalities of Congress. A further statement of the Chief Justice strengthens this view. "In cases brought to enforce constitutional rights," he said, "the judicial power of the United States necessarily extends to the independent determination of all questions, both of fact and law, necessary to the performance of that supreme function." Furthermore, "the essential independence of the exercise

[81] (1932), 285 U.S. 22, 56–57.

of the judicial power of the United States in the enforcement of constitutional rights requires that the Federal court should determine such an issue upon its own record and the facts elicited before it." [82]

In *St. Joseph Stockyards Co. v. United States*,[83] which involved the validity of rates chargeable by stockyards as fixed by the Secretary of Agriculture, the Court had occasion to reiterate the principles governing the decision in the *Crowell* case. Since legislative declarations or findings are "necessarily subject to independent judicial review upon the facts and the law by courts of competent jurisdiction to the end that the Constitution as the supreme law of the land may be maintained, the legislature cannot escape the constitutional limitation by authorizing its agent to make findings that the agent has kept within that limitation." Moreover, legislative agencies function in an atmosphere "peculiarly exposed to political demands," rather than in the rarefied atmosphere in which courts function, and are, therefore, incapable of rendering substantial justice even though it "is not difficult for them to observe the requirements of law in giving a hearing and receiving evidence." To say, however, "that their findings of fact may be made conclusive where constitutional rights of liberty and property are involved, although the evidence clearly establishes that the findings are wrong and constitutional rights have been invaded, is to place those rights at the mercy of administrative officials and seriously to impair the security inherent in our judicial safeguards." [84]

The general conclusion to be drawn from these cases is that Congress cannot withdraw from the judicial power

[82] *Ibid.*, 60, 64.   [83] (1936), 298 U.S. 38.   [84] *Ibid.*, 51–52.

vested in the regularly constituted courts of the United States any matter of private and constitutional right or "any matter which, from its nature, is the subject of a suit at the common law, or in equity, or admiralty," and vest it in any other agency either of Congress or of the executive. Such matters are included within the judicial power of the United States, a power, in some instances at least, in which legislative courts may neither share nor participate. Implicit in the *Crowell* and *St. Joseph Stockyards* cases, too, is the assumption of jurisdictional facts upon which constitutional rights may depend. Supremacy of the law is, therefore, judicial supremacy just as due process of law is judicial process.

Legislative courts, however, are not mere administrative agencies or divisions in the executive branch of the government. They are courts in the real sense of that term. They exercise judicial power; they afford an opportunity for notice and hearing; and they follow judicial procedure. Moreover, it is well settled that appellate review is not essential to due process of law but on the contrary is a matter of grace.[85] Again, as the Supreme Court said in *The Francis Wright:*

> Authority to limit the jurisdiction necessarily carries with it authority to limit the use of the jurisdiction. Not only may whole classes of cases be kept out of the jurisdiction altogether, but particular classes of questions may be subjected to re-examination and review, while others are not. . . . The general power to regulate implies the power to

[85] Luckenbach Steamship Co. v. U.S. (1926), 272 U.S. 533, 536; McKane v. Durston (1894), 153 U.S. 684, 687; Andrews v. Swartz (1895), 156 U.S. 272, 275; Reetz v. Michigan (1903), 188 U.S. 505, 508; The Francis Wright (1882), 105 U.S. 381, 386; Montana Co. v. St. Louis Mining and Milling Co. (1894), 152 U.S. 160, 171.

regulate in all things. The whole of a civil law appeal may
be given, or a part. The constitutional requirements are all
satisfied if one opportunity is had for the trial of all parts
of a case. Everything beyond that is matter of legislative discretion, not of constitutional right.[86]

The unrestrained exercise of power by Congress to
invest legislative courts with the final determination of
questions of fact and questions of law in all cases, however, would be an infringement not so much of the rights
protected by the guaranty of due process of law as an
encroachment upon the judiciary. Congress cannot "sap
the judicial power as it exists under the Federal Constitution." Congress' power to establish legislative courts,
therefore, does not extend beyond the necessity or propriety of such courts in the exercise of the powers delegated to Congress by the Constitution. Indeed, it is only
in the exercise of its delegated powers that Congress may
create special courts and "clothe them with functions
deemed essential or helpful in carrying those powers into
execution." [87]

Finally, the case of *Ex parte Bakelite Corporation* seems
to reiterate the distinction of matters arising between the
government and other parties which, from their nature,
do not require judicial determination, but are susceptible
of it, and matters of private determination by regularly
ordained constitutional courts. Among the matters included within this category are claims against the United
States, the valuation of imports for purposes of taxation,
and membership in Indian tribes. The first two of these
matters fall within the general categories of gratuities ex-

[86] (1882), 105 U.S. 381, 386, quoted with approval in Luckenbach
Steamship Co. v. U.S. (1926), 272 U.S. 533, 537.
[87] Ex p. Bakelite Corp. (1929), 279 U.S. 438, 449.

tended by the government and matters relating to the collection of the revenue. In each of these categories the courts have tended to extend to administrative officials the utmost latitude in disputes arising between the government and those upon whom it confers a boon, or from whom it seeks to collect taxes.

Suits brought to collect claims against the United States are purely a matter of grace to which any conditions, including finality of administrative determination, may be attached although, as a matter of fact, appeals to the Supreme Court are permitted.[88] The same is generally true of questions arising out of the administration of the customs laws. The individual has no inherent right to import goods into the country, and the efficient administration of the customs laws demands that the courts abstain from undue interference therewith. Accordingly, the creation of a customs court with power finally to determine such matters raises no constitutional questions.[89]

[88] The rules governing the extent of review by the Supreme Court of judgments of the Court of Claims were summarized in Luckenbach Steamship Co. v. U.S. (1926), 272 U.S. 533, 539. Where the findings of the Court of Claims are ambiguous, contradictory, or silent with respect to a material fact, or appear on their face to be ill-founded in point of law, the case will be remanded for further findings. However, mere assertion by a complainant that the findings are against the evidence, or are unsupported by it, is not sufficient cause for remanding the case, because this is to be done only when the necessity of correction of the decision or of additional evidence is apparent on the face of the findings or when they are examined in connection with the findings. Cf. U.S. v. Adams (1867), 6 Wall. 101, 110–112; Moore v. U.S. (1875), 91 U.S. 270; U.S. v. Smith (1877), 94 U.S. 214, 218; U.S. v. Clark (1878), 96 U.S. 37, 38; McClure v. U.S. (1885), 116 U.S. 145; Union Pacific R. Co. v. U.S. (1885), 116 U.S. 154; District of Columbia v. Barnes (1905), 197 U.S. 146, 150; Brothers v. U.S. (1919), 250 U.S. 88, 93.

[89] Auffmordt v. Hedden (1890), 137 U.S. 310; Hilton v. Merritt (1884), 110 U.S. 97; Passavant v. U.S. (1893), 148 U.S. 214; Cary v.

Similarly, the admission, expulsion, and naturalization of aliens present questions of a judicial nature that may be entrusted for final determination to a legislative or administrative court.[90] Here, again, the government is conferring a boon to which it may attach exceptions. Other matters arising in the administration of the affairs of government that may be entrusted to legislative courts for final determination are disputes arising out of patents,[91] controversies between the postal authorities and users of the postal service,[92] civil service cases, and the like.[93]

Indeed, the only limitations upon the power of Congress to establish legislative courts for the determination of matters to which the government is a direct party in interest are the necessary and proper clause and the judicial article. The limitations of the judicial article, as enunciated in *Murray v. Hoboken Land and Improvement Co.* and elaborated upon in *Crowell v. Benson*, absolutely prevent Congress from vesting matters of private right which might be a suit at the common law, or in

---

Curtis (1845), 3 How. 236; Bartlett v. Kane (1853), 16 How. 263. On the general question of administrative finality, see John Dickinson, *Administrative Justice and the Supremacy of Law in the United States* (Cambridge, 1927), chap. III.

[90] Fong Yue Ting v. U.S. (1893), 149 U.S. 698; U.S. v. Ju Toy (1905), 198 U.S. 253; Nishimura Ekiu v. U.S. (1892), 142 U.S. 651, 659, 660; Tutun v U.S. (1926), 270 U.S. 568.

[91] Butterworth v. U.S. ex rel. Hoe (1884), 112 U.S. 50; U.S. v. Duell (1899), 172 U.S. 576; Postum Cereal Co. v. California Fig Nut Co. (1927), 272 U.S. 693.

[92] Public Clearing House v. Coyne (1904), 194 U.S. 497; Houghton v. Payne (1904), 194 U.S. 88; Bates & Guild Co. v. Payne (1904), 194 U.S. 106; Smith v. Hitchcock (1912), 226 U.S. 53; Leach v. Carlile (1922), 258 U.S. 138. See also Lindsay Rogers, *The Postal Power of Congress* (*Johns Hopkins University in Historical and Political Science*, Series XXXIV, No. 2).

[93] Dickinson, *op. cit.*, 59.

equity, or admiralty in any but regularly constituted courts of the United States exercising the judicial power of the United States in the sense that this term is used in the third article of the Constitution. Otherwise, Congress has rather complete power to create administrative tribunals whenever such agencies are "necessary and proper" for executing the functions of the legislative and executive branches of government.

TABLE OF CASES

219

INDEX

This Index includes only those cases that have been discussed in the text.